That Sign of Perfection

That Sign of Perfection

From Bandy Legs to Beer Legs
Poems and Stories on the Game of Hockey

edited by John B. Lee

Black Moss Press

Published by Black Moss Press,
2450 Byng Road, Windsor, Ontario, N8W 3E8.
Black Moss Press books are distributed by
Firefly Books Ltd., 250 Sparks Avenue,
Willowdale, Ontario, M2H 2S4.
All orders should be directed there.

Financial assistance toward the publication of this book was provided
by the Department of Canadian Heritage, The Canada Council
and the Ontario Arts Council.

Cover art by A. Rossi, used with permission of *The Windsor Star*
Cover design by Richard Withey

Canadian Cataloguing in Publication Data:

That sign of perfection : from bandy legs to beer legs : poems and stories on the
game of hockey.

ISBN 0-88753-269-1

1. Hockey—Literary collections. 2. Canadian literature (english)—20th century. I.
Lee, John b., 1951-

PS8237.H6T48 1995   CB10.8'0355   C95-900509-9
PR9194.52.H6T48 1995

Acknowledgements

Roger Bell: "Come Back Jesus to the Hockey Game of Life" and "The Night the Arena Burned" from Mythtakes. (Midland: Whizzyfig Press, 1984). Reprinted by permission of the author.

C.H. (Marty) Gervais: "That Sign of Perfection" from Into A Blue Morning: Poems Selected and New 1968-1982. (Toronto: Hounslow Press, 1982). Reprinted by permission of the author.

Don Gutteridge: "When It Went Well" from Bus-Ride. (Alisa Craig, Ontario: Nairn Publishing, 1974) Reprinted by permission of the author. "Swallowing Pride" from God's Geography. (London, Ontario: Brick Books, 1982). Reprinted by permission of author and Brick Books.

Richard Harrison: "All Time Game," "The Feminine" and "The Sweater" from Hero of the Play. (Toronto: Wolsak & Wynn, 1994). Reprinted by permission of the author and Wolsak and Wynn Publishers Ltd.

Laurence Hutchman: "The Hockey Game" from Explorations. (Montreal: D.C. Books, 1975). Reprinted by permission of the author.

Gary Hyland: "Northland Pro" from Our Fathers. (Edmondton: Rowan, 1995). Reprinted by permission of the author.

M.T. Kelly: "A Puck in the Teeth" from This Magazine (XXVII). Reprinted by permission of the author.

John B. Lee: "Canine Pylons," "The Hockey Player Sonnets" and "When I Was a Boy and the Farm Pond Froze" from The Hockey Player Sonnets. (Ottawa: Penumbra, 1991). Reprinted by permission of the author and Penumbra Press.

Don Mckay: "Dreamskaters" and "Taking Your Baby to the Junior Hockey Game" from Birding, or desire. (Toronto: McClelland and Stewart, *The Canadian Publishers*, 1983). Reprinted by permission of the author.

Bruce Meyer: "Road Hockey" from Radio Silence. (Windsor, Ontario: Black Moss Press, 1993). Reprinted by permission of Black Moss Press.

Plantos: "Corner Man" from Mosquito Nirvana. (Toronto: Wolsak & Wynn, 1993). Reprinted by permission of the author.

Contents

A Puck in the Teeth

Small Histories in the Snow

Thin Ice

A Career In Hockey

for the love of the game

I see him in me, driving on,
searching for some hope of
perfection, that blazing instant
when skate blades glint
in the afternoon like
silver rockets & when the
black disc tumbles lightly
into the twine.

from *That Sign of Perfection*
C.H. (Marty) Gervais

from bandy legs to beer legs
from kids hacking it out between snow boot goals on ponds, gravel pits, frozen
creeks and backyard and schoolyard rinks
to old timers grinding it out in pickup games in the late night arenas of little
towns and big cities all across the country and for all the glory between
for the players with plenty of heart and soft hands
for the pylons and hackers who keep going though they have nothing to give but
their love of the game
for the fathers and mothers up by five and out by six on the coldest morning of
the winter
for their sons and daughters—
from wobble-skaters with their kitchen chairs to showboats and sharpshooters
for the netminders, for the blueliners, the centres and wings
for the spectators who watch and for the players who play
for what we remember and what we dream
this is hockey

A Puck in the Teeth

A Puck in the Teeth

M.T. Kelly

There was a new smell, a cold arena odour of gas from the Zamboni, of mould and damp, french fries and maybe the hint of a urinal. My son was trying out for a hockey team in the Metropolitan Toronto Hockey League (MTHL), I was about to become a serious hockey parent, and I realized that I had never been in a place like this in my life.

This was Chesswood, four rinks in one building, described by another new hockey father, an Australian, as a dump. There was ugly energy in the warm central part of the complex, as children in team jackets and teenagers with shaved heads clustered around video games. They pushed and shoved, wrestled restlessly, careless of other people, or stared intently at fighting on the screens. Out front, Jaguars and Mercedes were parked alongside beat-up Buick Skylarks; shiny jeeps and vans stood out beside rusted Toyotas. All the cars were surrounded by deliquescing soft drink cups, tinfoil, shattered pavement. There was money and crumminess and dedicated purpose here; investment and ambition.

My son had brought me to this. He was the one who had heard about the MTHL while playing "house league," the one who wanted to try out, move up, get beyond "all stars" and "selects." I supported him, and entered a world that would not only take up a lot of time and money, but would overturn beliefs and prejudices I had held since childhood. It was a world that would confirm biases and be fraught with mixed emotions; a world where parents could confuse their own identity with that of their children.

The place, with its scum on rubber mats, puck-streaked glass and dim hallways, made me afraid. All too easily I could imagine, even smell the copper of blood, see a lax broken ankle or hanging dislocated shoulder, understand the wait for an ambulance with dirt on the floor, knowing a season, a career, might be over. This is the kind of place it happened, I feared, the worst—hit from behind by some indifferent goon. Paralysis.

My son certainly wasn't thinking about wheel-chairs. He didn't even play contact yet. But the ambience of Chesswood made vivid my prejudices. Hockey had always made me feel like an alien in my own country. It looked as if that was going to continue. The things I had been good at as a kid, and as an adult, were never as valued as hockey was. Now I was about to be confirmed even more strongly as an outsider.

My feelings would change dramatically, although I would retain an adult ambivalence about the competitive hockey culture and how it made children feel. But my son loved hockey, he had a deep connection to what I had never had, and I let him have it, marvelling at all I found new. After those first tryouts I heard a father in the dressing room, as worried as I was, ask his son, "You okay kid? The coach okay? He seems to yell a lot."

"I love it," the boy said. "I love it, I love it, I love it. He's so insensitive!"

The kid's comment seemed to me to be about hockey, doing the thing itself, not ideas of what you were supposed to feel about the sport. I'd try to be a little "insensitive," to get beyond first impressions, to see what was before me and not what I expected to see.

Very early, hockey had become, for me, a metaphor about being left out. Where I came from in Toronto, first the Junction, then Parkdale, the hockey myth was not in much evidence as far as I was concerned. I had no father, so no father could help me with my shot; the main sport of the men I knew was drinking. There were no outdoor ponds (in fact, no kind of "ice-time") where you could dream of greatness. There was certainly no money for equipment.

I was exposed to the sport, however, during my tenure at a private Catholic boys' school (my aunt paid the fees—it was felt I would do better with the violent Christian brothers after my father died), where we got to use the rink. Anyone who could even skate, came from places with names like Leaside and Rosedale. They all seemed to have two parents, money, and not to live in apartments.

The one hockey experience that I remember more than any other, that would colour how I viewed the sport, was dealt by a kid from Rosedale.

15

Don't think I wasn't acutely aware of where he came from. It made what he did significant, driving home all that I lacked.

What happened on that outdoor rink, in the sun of a winter morning so long ago, that made me hate hockey? It is easy enough to say I can still see the puck coming up after it was shot at me—see it come to this day, its black oval against the expanse of the ice, the arc in the achingly white morning light. The puck was shot deliberately, at least I think so, and knocked the wind out of me. But as I lay curled up on the ice, feeling sorry for myself, gasping, I knew I had reason to hate the kid, and his kind, who could do this to me. Them. I was Excluded, and I got hurt.

It wasn't that I didn't like sports, though I only became really good at some of them once I hit puberty and had an opportunity, at a different school, to participate. I'd always liked boxing, and kept scrapbooks of fighters. One of the few men who was nice to me when I was a kid was Steve Rocco, ex-contender for the flyweight championship of the world. (Besides, boxing is a lonely writer's sport; you don't have to get along with other boys, with teammates, to do it.) I'd say I met Mr. Rocco five times. But he was a man, and he let me sit and fish with him at Lake Simcoe. Mr. Rocco had great dignity and kindness, and I will never forget him.

On leaving De La Salle (a kid got punched full in the face by Brother Xavier when he said he was "going steady" —it was time to escape), I went to Parkdale Collegiate where there were girls, a symphony orchestra instead of a drum and bugle corps, and track and field and swimming instead of hockey and football. But the sports I excelled in, such as track, didn't have the mass tribal appeal that football and hockey did. It was not the same kind of team. As a defensive measure, I had to feel superior to the guys on hockey and football teams.

My prejudice grew. When I first started trying to get published, I was jolted by a shock recognition when I read an article called "Home Truths," in Northern Journey, a literary magazine, in which Fraser Sutherland said that there had to be more to life than a "puck in the teeth." He was championing the efforts of his mother, and other farm wives in rural Nova Scotia, who bravely supported the arts in communities where they were not generally as valued as hockey talent.

Later, when the Philadelphia Flyers reigned supreme, I couldn't even watch hockey on TV at a friend's house. Here was a clumsy medieval morality play, except that the bad guys always won, and they won by gang-bullying and bashing. It was to be years before I was exposed to hockey and saw another side to its physical nature, one that was not dirty and brutal, and heard the word "heart" used to describe hockey players.

Now, my child has this nearly obsessive attachment to hockey. He loves it. After his first few games, watching the kids come on in waves in their brilliant uniforms, I loved it too. Very quickly, I got caught up in the syndrome of nearly every parent whose son gets really involved in competitive hockey: I lived and died by his ice time.

A year later, I heard the phenomenon explained this way, "It's narcissism. You put so much into the kid, your own feelings, things that aren't right with your life, that you feel if he doesn't perform well, your own ego will die."

That's a good insight, but I don't know about it in the beginning, and because of the nature of hockey—it is a blood sport, in that it stirs the blood, arouses the feelings like few other sports—I jumped into the role of hockey parent with, shall we say, unseemly vigour.

"GET UP." I would have the impulse to shout if my son fell. "GET ON 'EM!" This after trying to play the game myself and winding up coughing for half an hour after one shift. The urge did not abate, no matter how much reason was brought to bear. "Is that all you remember about the game?" my son asked once as I pointed out, compulsively, I really couldn't stop myself, one of his mistakes.

I know I'm better now, because he told me that I'm "not a hockey father anymore." Still, I have my lapses. In a close game in which my son received a "questionable" penalty with less than a minute to go, I bellowed out "BULLSHIT." My vow to be quiet, which I had kept for nearly a year, went quickly away when all the myriad disappointments of that particular Sunday, not to say life, were focused by the game and directed at the referee. Afterward, my son chastened me: "You mustn't swear."

This dangerous identification can be controlled, but you have to know it's going on. Then hockey can teach a kind of restraint, along with engendering great enthusiasm. My son has changed my mind about the game. Much of what I had felt about hockey was received opinion reinforced by my early experiences. I almost feel a victim of ideology, reflexively shaking my head in agreement and tut-tutting about outrages that are not going on.

Of course, there is a lot wrong with hockey, and I still have adult ambivalent feelings. What is corrupt in the sport has been well documented. In his compelling new book, Road Games, Roy MacGregor, who genuinely loves hockey and understands it, brilliantly shows the greed and venality present in the NHL, a place so many kids dream about. And at a recent "Festival of Friendship" tournament in Cambridge, Ontario, I saw "meathead" hockey with kids of 13 that was so gratuitously violent and dirty that it resulted in a broken ankle (slashed from behind with seven seconds to go) that made me certain I would march down on the ice and withdraw my son—probably to his chagrin—if he was ever in such a game.

But so far, he has not been in such a game. I don't think I'm simply naive in hoping the MTHL is sincere when it issues bulletins against "cowardly" hitting from behind. What has actually gone on since my son started playing is different than I expected. There has been no violence of the extreme kind I worried about. Sure, hockey is a rough game, but I have been all set to bemoan what has not happened.

Received opinions were thrown aside. Almost reflexively, I found myself ready to talk about the superiority of graceful, European-style hockey. Yet my son plays "Canadian" hockey. He's a big kid, and that counts for something; yet I was ready from the first tryouts to side with the parents of smaller children, the advocates of another style. It took more than a moment to stop and look at what was before me; being bigger than your opponent might not be fair in the cosmic scheme of things but sometimes, only sometimes, it gives you an advantage. I had trouble accepting the advantage.

My son has had a bad coach, an ineffective coach and a good coach, but in a core way, the bad experiences have not affected his enjoyment of hockey, or mine. In spite of the "politics," hockey has provided a forum in which an unambiguous, impersonal standard can determine things. There is how you play, and you can do it or you can't. And if you can't, nobody says you're a better or a worse person than those who can. It's something that's clear.

Hockey parents? There is much that is distressing: A mother bangs frantically on the glass to get her ten-year-old's attention. "Play tough, Kevin. Play mean." But an important moment in the relationships of parents to kids, and an insight about the nature of sport, came to me in a father-son game.

I had been to the surgical-supply outlet the day before, and had more iron in the brace on my right leg than Robo-Cop. Out on the ice, I stood in front of the kids' net and circled, hoping to get free of Pino, the smallest player on the team, 65 pounds maybe, who was covering me closely. Pino leaned his weight against me, as he'd been taught—contact is being initiated at this level. When the puck came out I whacked (slashed) Pino.

Yikes! "Sorry, Pino," I said. "You okay? Sorry."

"No problem, Mr. Jonah," Pino said. (My son's name is Jonah. Pino didn't know my name.) "No problem, man; don't worry about it." And he skated away. Quickly. It was all very fast, but I caught the smile.

That kind of connection, the kids smiling, giving elfin grins at the same time as they give you a shot, happened a lost in that game. Such intimacy at such speed. (Intimacy is a dangerous, loaded word these days, and I fear using it. But a friend said, "Boxing is intimate, you know that." So I'll use it. High spirits, friendliness, doesn't get it; sometimes, friendliness has nothing to do with it.)

During that father-son game, I saw how close hockey players can be to each other, yapping away, "hitting" and I saw how much many parents really wished their kids well. Hockey became a two-edged sword, a metaphor with many resonances, and not just mine.

If I go back to that raised puck when I was a boy—what did it mean, aside from the sociology and grievances I attached to it? Well, winter spoke as I lay gasping on the ice, and the high clear sky let me know it didn't care. But that very indifference carried reassurance. There was the sweep of ice; there was, beyond the boards of the rink, gravel glinting in the too bright morning sun; lawns rolling away and covered with snow. Hockey had taken me outside into the weather, just as I, occasionally, got outside my classroom and home. There was simply the moment in the wonderful cold. It is what was crystal in that day, and the days of those seasons, that I remember. Winter really was separate from the hellish maelstrom of my home and school life.

It is all too easy to say the outdoor rink at the Exhibition Grounds was a place to go and get into fights, to worry about getting into fights, to act "rangy" on ice so you wouldn't have to get into fights, or to meet girls.

What remains is the liquid metal expanse of Lake Ontario heaving in the cold. Huge, bigger than anything, slate and molten except in the rare moments the sun was out. And black mould frozen in the boards of the change hut; the splintery stained boards. Hockey brought me back to that. There was a hint of the cold vastness of the country.

Rinks can still do this, even if they're indoors and smell differently and are in North York, and if what goes on in them is highly organized. Once you leave the sealed hot shouting of an arena on a winter night and go home under the stars, it is impossible not to be aware of where you are. The same feeling can happen in spring—playoffs!—when twilight is lavender and the air humid and close. The changing seasons don't alter the intense emotion of the game, but awareness of those seasons is heightened, by the bag heavy with sweat, the kid's smiling face after a workout, the air as you open the door to go outside, and to something outside you, again.

Small Histories in The Snow

Playing Hockey on Crang's Pond

Laurence Hutchman

We dreamed of playing at the Gardens
waited for *Hockey Night in Canada* following
the *Plouffe Family, Don Messer's Jubilee, Tommy Hunter,*
waited for the Ford to drive into the gas station
to the chorus of the Esso anthem:
"What a great feeling, what a wonderful sight
of sheer enjoyment and of confidence..."
7:00 Saturday mornings we played
house league hockey on the windy ice of Roding Rink
keeping warm by jumping up and down on the bench.

Sometime at the end of the fifties in our own cold war
the place to play hockey was at Crang's Pond.
After school we gathered up schoolbags, skates and sticks
and trudged a half-mile along Vero Beach Boulevard
playing bonkers in the waist-high fields
until we reached the pond, large as a lake
where the Crang's Tudor Mansion looked down on us.

We played with the Vogel brothers, Stewart, O'Connor
tightening skates on the frozen banks
striding onto the ice, clearing the rink and choosing sides.
Each game was different:
the swerves, the deeks, glides, passing and shooting
to break through the defence
the breakaway...bearing down on the goalie
(the way I saw Belliveau or Mahovlich move)
aiming for a corner by the boot post into the snow net.
After the breathy exhaustion of the sudden death goal
we left our indecipherable signatures on the dark ice.

That year we tried to prolong the hockey season
already the water lapped the reedy pond's edge.
It was so warm I took off my coat and gloves
and the ice split not far from us
getting softer and turning a little gold,
coloured from seeping water and sunshine.
And we played the game into the warm afternoon until
the whole damned pond sagged and cracked beneath us.

I remember the last time that we played
the end of the championship season
in the Downsview Beaver House League.
Our goalie Dickie Stanley told us
he was moving to Arizona because of his mother's allergies.
Next year, I imagined him taking his goalie pads
from the pick-up, carrying them through the desert parking lot
into the cool emptiness of the Phoenix Arena, and once again
suiting up with us on Crang Pond's glinting ice.

Boy

Mark Cochrane

Cathy says:
You are always using the word
but you never say what it means to you.

Richard says:
This is my hockey. Did you ever see me play it?

I say:
I hate the father, but I love my dad.

Desperate for something but relieved at nothing
I bowed my head, I waited & waited
for a crop of hair, dark nimbus
to appear
& blot the white
chub of my pubis.

It was the one page I could not write, by will.

At twelve I quit the city "A" league
when smaller boys
with their compact torsion
began to lay me flat. I was big
but soft, sweat not pungent, not yet musk,
& worst of all
I was glad for that.

Trace to this moment if you must,
my fear of shower-rooms & locker chat.

O pupae, O the smooth & featureless.
Grown men, the emissions of their skins,
revulsed me, & like (& unlike) a girl too thin
& wanting to be thinner, breastless, I dreaded
metamorphosis.

Every story of the adulthood of my body
begins the year I quit hockey clean, without muscle, &

when puberty finally came, I was fourteen,
it was too late. Manhood already knew
I was a traitor to its form.

But desire doubles back on disgust.
Now I'm back in the game with other men
& can hardly tell repulsion, or jealousy, from lust.

The homoerotic? I consume the other man in mind
to become him, sculpted & buffed
to a sheen, my ideal self in the imagined
eyes of women. (Oh, that's one disavowal..

O Daddy, O Daedalus, O magician:
because I could never measure up to your body
or your idea of it, brute & heavy
but perfectible, tight & sexed for flight,

because I could never harden myself
to the sleekness of a rooster & rise,

I nearly drowned in a refusal
of the wings you had invented, I nearly proved
that the impressionable son
melts.

*

25

My dad, in the autumn of his seventeenth year,
was on the cusp of making
the major-junior team in Moose Jaw

(& everything that promised)

when he took a football cleat in the calf
& lost the season of both sports.

Where I come from
athletics are a man's first career.
Any other life
is a rebellion or a compromise
based on the failure to make pro.

Yesterday in the community centre
I stepped onto the rink, wet & bluish
like the white of an eye
after the Zamboni run.

That smell, *air of the ice,* it hit me
like a shoulder to the lungs:

I am six years old & taking a face-off

at five-thirty in the morning my dad
is a bushy bear
with a seventies haircut
& his moustache in the steam—

he is smiling over coffee—

a warm
rush of reassurance
from his cupped hands of prayer
in the stands.

*

This spring, after many apart, we attend
NHL games
like therapy, like
devotions, the arcana
& arithmetic of the sportspage
a way of talking.

As fathers, as dads, we are only beginning
to find a way back, through men
& their measures,
to the meaning of a boy
& the soft, muscular care
he was born to.

When I Was a Boy and the Farm Pond Froze

John B. Lee

When I was a boy
once every winter the farm pond froze
wide as a field from fence to fence
we'd go down with skates, puck and stick
and play in the burning wind for days
the ice slithering with cracks
under our weight
seeping at first with water, then
collapsing in dried hollows where the furrows
cut tiny valleys
in the plough-rolled earth
till the game shrunk to such boundaries
of ruin
we could hardly turn between the evaporating kingdoms
of snow-boot goals.
Then one terrible day the whole wreckage
broken on the knuckles of frosted clods
would lie fallen like a puzzle tossed in the air.
That was the last of the generous mornings.
The last of the pond
groaning like a fat man's bed
when the wind turned suddenly cold and ordinary
and the snow scattered in filthy patches
stippled with dust.

Chicken Legs

Hugh MacDonald

He's a big guy
ten years old
Atom double A
Amid the clatter slap bang
of the white boards
he's a flying boxcar
crashing end to end.
Capture, pass, chase
check, check, check
watch the off sides
go to the net
get out! get out!
He can shoot now
Neighbours can hear it
from outside the rink.
Ties his own skates
lugs his own gear
spits on the floor.
"I wish we could check in Atom,"
he says in the dressing room.
"Did you see me clothes-line that guy?"
Looks from team-mate to mother
(who frowns at the alien
growing inside her baby)
removes skates and pads.
The little monster
stands shrunken on chicken legs
packs most of himself
into his musty hockey bag.

Behind the Red Brick House

Charlottetown, P.E.I. 1955

Hugh MacDonald

Doctor Joe and Colin
and the twins
stand in soggy sleeves
behind the house
They lay the water down
in shining pools
night after night
and on frost crisp mornings
break up shells
of tinkle ice
that mar the thickening surface
then melt it down
with steaming floods
and leave for the office and school
impatient for the work to end

Soon come nights
when hordes of children
shove inside the changing shed
fill lungs with kerosene charged air
or sit and wheeze
and tie their skates
on ice-lump mounds
along the edge

Captains toss
an out-of-season bat
pick shouting teams
and nets are coats
or hunk of snow

With eyes like young owls
we stick handle
around figure-skating girls
and flirting pairs
"no lifties" is the rule
but pucks still fly
we scramble over banks
and mine mounds of drift

We play till toes are trapped
laces locked in hanging icicles
We're never more awake
than when we leave
and crunch along streets
sticks across shoulders
hobo style
our skates
lace-hung and steaming
at our backs
and once in bed
we sleep so fast
and dream
of how we'll play
the next game
and the next

Skating Against Sin

C.H. (Marty) Gervais

They built a skating rink
back of the seminary
in London, Ontario
—pine boards and
chicken wire goalie nets—
where the young men scrapped
on the ice in what was left
of day time after dreary
afternoons of theology
And when darkness set in
they'd switch on
what few floodlights
there were to eke out
a few more hours
till night prayers
beckoned them back
to the sanctuary
and those small narrow
rooms to ponder
the dynamics of sin

My Father Must Have Taught Me to Skate

Susan Helwig

My father must have taught me to skate
but I can't remember
he must have wrapped his arms around my waist
urged me forward on buckled, hurting ankles
but I have no memory of this;
surely he took me up in fatherly embrace
carried me off the ice when I cried,
or even at five, did I know not to?
My father must have taught me to skate
for now I can cut a perfect figure eight,
waltz when I have a partner
impossible to have learned by myself;
My father must have taught me to skate
yet I cannot recall
now I see only what my body knows:
a solitary glide
and hands that reach out
for balance.

New Skates

C.H. (Marty) Gervais

When I see my young son pulling
on a pair of stiff new skates, I remember
a time just after Dief got elected
and we had moved to the north
and all my new friends were getting ready
for hockey season, and I had never played hockey
except on a road with running shoes
and a net made of potato sacks
At first, there was pride in watching my father
sharpen skates in the basement —sparks flying
about like fireflies—With great satisfaction,
he handed us those soft leather black ankle skates
that he had salvaged from an old cardboard box
found under the basement stairs
before we had left Windsor
and polished them army boot clean
and told us that by sharpening them himself
he had saved 25 cents at the arena
Said he could do just as good a job himself
But the edges were rough and uneven
and, predictably, we fell flat on our asses
on the ice as our friends circled about us—
their laughter falling around us
as we silently cursed our father
who was down at the plant working
oblivious to our humiliation
We didn't tell him anything
because he would have yanked the skates
away from us and worked on them
until they felt sharp against his thumb
and we knew that wouldn't do any good

and he would have told us to get the polish
out and give them a good shine
but nobody ever polished skates
It was my mother who finally
carried the skates over to the skate shop
and learned from the owner
nobody wore skates like that anymore—
in fact he hadn't seen any skates like that
since before the Second World War—
no ankle support and the leather so worn
that it was smooth as a glove,
and told her that somebody could get hurt with these
especially playing hockey
Reluctantly she bought us each a new pair
I remember running my hand over
the smooth leather and the hard toe
of the skates—they seemed
perfectly formed, so fast
And all we needed now to save face
was to keep skating, to keep my father away
from the blades, to keep skating, never
to look behind, to keep right on moving

The Mouse in the Christmas Pageant

Karen Mulhallen

It began with the road apples
it was a country town
and the milkwagons came down from Silverwoods Dairy
at the top of Canterbury street
and there were horses snorting in the cold air
and exhalations,
and urictations
and the stirrups of the wagons were strapped on like shin guards
with leather traces
and pads, and blinds on their eyes.

The milk would be frozen and the cream top bulging out from under the
cardboard sealer in the glass bottles at the back door

and the boys would go out
with their sticks and their brooms
and whackwhacka whack
and the banks of snow were tall
and fresh
and we shivered
our lips blue

but it was good for us we knew
the fresh air
the bright cheeks
and the icecold milk waiting
just inside the outside kitchen door.

There is something about the arena
at the back of the firehall
it's cold there too

and the boys are strapping on their pads
and putting on their helmets
and everyone wishes they had a dime
for the hot chocolate made with water
and the little girls shiver in their wood-plank dressing room
while the boys go out and switch about, cutting up the ice
with their broad blades, and the parents sit up on the bleachers
drinking the chocolate water
rooting for their boys, who swish by in helmets and sweaters,
banging their pucks against the boards
slap into the net, against the goal posts
against the huge gloves
and caged eyes of the goal
and then the magic moment
when the ice is cleared
and a waltz of some kind rattles over the tinny speakers
and a stream of little girls emerges from their chilly leanto
little limbs shake in the fawn tights, forming a line
and they begin to follow the lead girl,
who is more golden than the others
around and around the ice, cut up by the boys trained on road
apples
the girls skate back wards and forwards
their little pony tails dance,
bangs bow, pirouette, twist, fall, and it's up again

the first magic of being other,
the short skirt in tartan cut in a complete circle
the little jacket, the gangly fawn limbs
the flip of bangs, and toss of the tail.

I'm there too of course, one of the mice in the Cinderella pageant
the cold war has begun, the boys are eager to take the puck all the
way
from southern Ontario to Korea.

It's not our war but we wish it were, think it is,
and we all shiver and make lists:
Mirror mirror on the wall,
Who's the fairest of them all?

There are no parents watching the mice
in their silver blades
it's gender territory and mice are
only brooches on the pads of guys in Charles Atlas costumes
and none of my brothers are out on the ice—no way
in a sensitive family
boys play music, and write
and fight their way outside of road apple territory.

After the rehearsals for pageants and hockey
there was always Lamont's bakery,
and the snow, the snow by the side of the road,
by the side of Main Street
the snow on the way to the baker, to Lamont's bakery
and the snow in the alley with the horses at Dawes Bakery
where faun-haunched Peter Dawes, the town idiot,
locked the little girl in the stable
fondling road apples on his mind
after the game of road apples
after the chocolate water

the mouse in fawn tights
crosses her legs and lines up

and the donuts there so big
and the road so long and the snow at the sides
so high, and no other day was quite like that day,
or so the poet said, or so the poets say

a moment for a deal, a little coin exchange
the donuts were so big, the snow was so high
the sugar was so sweet
the buns so hot
and outside the door the steady stream of pee
while the boys trooped by
road apples on their minds.

And only a moment until
Bill and I, in his old red MG TD,
unlike any other car on the road apple road
were bouncing its wooden frame down those country lanes
in road apple land off the skyscrapers of snow.

You think this is where it all ends
the country mouse
in her fawn tights,
her sensitive brothers, like cruel stepsisters,
but that isn't the way it went at all.

The Queen of Cottam Pond: A Memoir

Lisa Kulisek

As a grown-up, I haven't felt the urge to skate in a very long time and I haven't seen the old pond in years. I'm usually too busy now in winter to think about enjoying the cold weather. But when I was young, I dreamed of wearing an oversized jersey and skating into the sunset.

I remember buying my first and only pair of skates. They were called figure skates, and they were white, because girls couldn't wear hockey skates. I also remember the socks my mom bought for me that same day in Essex. They were blue woolies with white toes and stripes—"Boys Socks" branded in black and white right there on the side.

The surface of Cottam Pond where we played would be transformed into our own personal olympic ice. For the kids who lived nearby, it was a place of our own, and with a little help from the volunteer fire department who would flood it to smooth out the bumps and fill in the cracks, it became perfect. A couple of older boys with snow shovels performed the sacred rite of Zamboni and the Rotary club Christmas lights that stayed up year-round set the mood.

Walking on skate guards we trekked to the picnic table next to the pond. There were rocks used for markers round the pond edge. If you could clamber over them in a graceful fashion, or better yet, get a running start and jump them, your admission was assured. I remember the delicious sound and feel of my skate blades on the cold hard rock. I used to fight the guilt about dulling my blades just to hear that scritch-tink sound.

The day I got my first and only hockey stick from Canadian Tire in Essex, I waved it around and felt like the Queen of Cottam Pond. However, since I was a girl, I was often in the one net and one of the girls I'd convinced to play for a short time was usually in the other net. We didn't have the right skates. She didn't have her own stick. We were seen as "too fragile" to be in the fray. I was, after all, just a girl. "Keep it on the ice, the girls are playing, no slapshots!"

I don't remember how we set up times to play there, but Sundays were for sure, and any other time during winter break there were almost always enough kids around to make a game. My greatest moment came on the glorious day I was checked so hard that I flew off the ice, over the rocks that ringed the pond, and into the snow on the other side. I'd finally made it. I was playing hockey! I gained a certain respect that day from my fellow players, after they stopped the game and picked me up, making sure I was okay.

Over the years, the numbers dwindled on our little pond. The few girls who played saw that their efforts were futile. There were no "real girl hockey players." Girls just sat in the stands and watched and dreamed of wearing an ill-fitting jersey with someone else's name on it. My own hockey days were over for good when I broke the blade off my stick. Before the next winter, the next frozen pond, I had grown out of my figure skates, too.

But don't be too surprised if some day you come across a woman in black hockey skates with a broken stick raised over her head and a glazed look in her eyes cheering another one "right in the net."

Small Histories in the Snow

Roger Bell

We wrote our small histories
in the snow with sticks
taped and patched
held together by dreamsglue

in the streets where cars dared not
all the boys like black crows flocked
to clack and whack
at the frozen eye of winter

mornings till the big bell called us
noons after gulping scalds of soup
after 4 as the light gave out, grey
and often, softer, after dark
in the shadowland of houselights
flecked with falling clouds

each time we left we didn't
we left our laughter

      and
we left our wooden surrogates
to hold our place
we left our sticks angled
into banks jammed and tossed
like random runes that only we
returning to the fray
like young Arthurs could extract
and interpret into action
there on that smooth
and endless stretch of road

Road Hockey

Bruce Meyer

The middle of my journey,
as the train shakes,
I wake from a dream
about my childhood
where I saw the boys
I played hockey with
on the frozen streets
beneath purple dusks.
Snow had settled
on the brown furrows
of the fall ploughings
the way a dusting of ice
clung to our corduroys
as we shouted and raved
in a dead-end street,
pushing and hacking
each other's spindly legs
until the night descended
blackening the game
and calling us home
to those tiny rooms
taped with clippings
of Howe and Hull
and silver grails.
I wanted to go back there,
wanted to dream again
of what I would become
but only became
the things I am
regardless of the dreams.
And as I woke just now,

at some point in a journey
I realized we'd all
become grown men,
and the waking, not the growing
left me angry. Snow whirls
by the coach car window,
still clings to the furrows
of pantlegs and fields
as the journeymen continue on
their battles of earthly overtime
and the sudden darkness
after.

The Shut Out

Delores Reimer

"Get away from me, shithead!"

Fiona was trying to dipsy doodle away from Bob. They had been playing street hockey since just after supper. The score was 10-10. The street light by Doug's house created an umbrella of light making the boundary of their playing area a circle. It was Fiona, Kenny, and Doug against Phil, Bobby and Gary.

"Fiona, your Mom's here," Phil said as he picked the puck off her stick. He dodged Kenny, stick handling his way to where Gary stood with his goalie stick protecting a space between two coffee cans filled with ice near the edge of the light circle.

Fiona turned to look. There she was. Navy parka unzipped, slippers on her feet, no gloves and her arms moving up and down like crow's wings in summer. "Caw caw caw" thought Fiona watching Jacqueline's mouth move up and down, not hearing the words. She took off her toque.

"Come here Fiona, right this minute."

'I could run...straight down this street to the highway and on and on.' She knew she was in trouble. She walked to her mother.

"Fiona Louise, that was no way for a lady to talk! I knew as soon as I saw you out here playing hockey again you'd be using strong language. A lady doesn't curse. Get in the house right now. You're too old to play with boys! Put that stick down and go finish your homework."

Fiona looked at Jacqueline. How did I ever end up with her as a mother, she wondered, looking at how green her skin appeared in the streetlight? She looked like an old martian with her face screwed up in the *disapproval* look, her mouth coloured with Avon's Poppy Red lipstick. The white vapour from her hot breath hitting the outside air evaporated above her head the way cigarette smoke dissipated in air. Fiona watched as it floated above and disappeared against the dark sky. The sour smell

45

of Jacqueline's breath wafted towards her.

"Phil," Fiona raised her voice. "Thanks for the stick."

"See you tomorrow Fiona."

"Yeah, see you."

Fiona shoved the butt end into the snowbank and turned to follow her mother home. She heard the boys giggle and a falsetto "Ladies don't talk like that." Then more laughter. She had never felt so embarrassed in her life.

"Really Fiona, girls don't play hockey, and you shouldn't play with boys anymore. What are people like Mr. and Mrs. Baker going to think?" Jacqueline opened the door and let Fiona walk into the house before her.

"Mom, I was just playing hockey."

"But that will lead to other things and you'll get a reputation for being fast. Ladies don't hang around with boys and they don't talk the way I heard you speak out there. You're grounded for a week. No staying with Brenda on the weekend."

"Mom, that's not fair. There is nothing to do in the house in the winter." Fiona took off her parka and hung it in the closet, then put her mitts on the hot air register so they would be dry in the morning.

"Fiona, shut your mouth and don't talk back. The boys won't have respect for you if you play hockey with them. In the end, when all is said and done, they won't treat you like a lady—they'll be too familiar and you won't have any mystique. Besides, I don't want you hanging around with that Phil. He's trouble, I hear." Her eyes narrowed. "What else has been happening out there?"

"Nothing."

"I hope none of them have tried to kiss you."

"Mom! We just play hockey."

"No more. I forbid you to play. No daughter of mine is going to hang around boys and ruin her reputation. Now get to your room. I don't want to see you anymore tonight. And don't forget, you're grounded."

The next morning it was still dark when Fiona walked to the bus stop. Kenny, Bobby, Phil, and Doug were huddled in a circle smoking.

"Fiona," Phil said and nodded.

"Did you catch shit last night?" Kenny asked.

"A bit," she said. "Look, I'm really sorry. But, uh, is the big game against George and his gang still on for Sunday night?"

"THE BUS IS COMING! THE BUS IS COMING!" Bobby's little brother David yelled. The boys dropped their smokes and passed around a pack of Wrigley's Doublemint before Mr. Butcher could catch them smoking.

"Uh, yeah," said Doug, looking at the ground. "But we don't want you to play anymore. Your Mom makes trouble for us with our folks. Sorry."

"You're good for a girl," Kenny said. "And maybe we need another player, but we can't have your mom stopping the game on Sunday."

Fiona could hardly see the steps of the bus when she climbed aboard. She felt foolish with her eyes full of tears. Blindly she found her friend Brenda, who always saved her a seat.

"You're lucky to have the same bus stop as Phil. He's so cute. Can you come to my house and do homework tonight?"

"No. I'm grounded."

"What did you do?"

"Nothing. Just played hockey. I think she heard me swearing."

"Mothers are B-I-T-C-H-es," said Brenda. "Look at the ugly pants mine made me wear."

Fiona pressed the tip of her index finger on the frosty bus window and watched as a clear space melted. She blew on it until it was large enough to look out of and watched the trees and buildings go by. She looked out the window, making her peephole bigger and bigger while the school girls sang their repertoire of Petula Clark's Downtown; Found a Peanut; Diana Ross; and Nancy Sinatra.

Fiona sang quietly along with them.

These boots are made for walking
And that's just what they'll do
One of these days, these boots are gonna
Walk all over you.

Fiona thought this was a funny song. On the Ed Sullivan Show, Nancy Sinatra was wearing white go-go boots and everyone on the bus was wearing brown or black snow boots. She pictured snow boots possessed by the Devil walking by themselves over people.

"Brenda, do you ever feel like running away?" Fiona turned from the window.

"Yeah, when my Mom's a real bitch and it seems like I can't do anything right."

The bus pulled up to Scott Junior High.

"See you after school," Brenda said as they climbed off the bus.

Fiona stood where the bus left them and watched as Phil and the boys and Brenda and the rest of the kids walked into the school. She looked down the road. I could just walk and walk and walk and keep going on and on forever. No one would miss me. She looked across the street at the arena. "Girls don't play Hockey. It's unladylike to sweat," she mimicked. "Ladies wear dresses, why do you want to wear those pants? Keep your knees together..." The buzzer rang. She turned and ran for the front doors of the school.

***

"Hey Dad, wouldn't it be great to play in the NHL?"

Fiona and Peter were making popcorn. It was Saturday night. Hockey Night in Canada was on TV. Peter was pouring melted butter over the bowl of popped corn.

"It's nice to know I have a date every Saturday night in the winter." Peter winked at her.

Fiona just grinned and handed Peter his rye and coke. She took a sip of her orange juice.

"Where's the rooster?" he asked.

"Who?"

"The rooster...your mother."

Fiona stared, puzzled, at Peter.

"Don't you think she reminds you of a rooster in the morning with her hair standing on end and all that crowing?"

"Not with that hair." Peter downed half his drink and topped it up with rye. "Come on, let's go watch the game. Boston and Toronto, my girl."

"Boston's my favourite team." Fiona sat on the floor in front of the television.

"Is Bobby Orr your favourite hockey player?"

"No. Derek Sanderson."

"Aahh, he's a goon."

"Oh Dad! He's real cute, and when he skates his hair blows behind him. Brenda thinks he's cute too. Shelly likes Bobby Orr, but Brenda and I think he's too baby-faced."

"Peter really, you shouldn't be encouraging her about this hockey business."

"Hey Jackie, what's the big deal? A lot of women like hockey."

"She wants to play."

"It's impossible for girls to play, so don't worry about it. Leave the girl alone. There's no harm done."

"YES! Cheevers stopped him." Fiona cheered.

"Fiona! Don't yell in the house." Jacqueline spoke firmly as she zipped up her jacket.

"Say hello to Joyce for me. Look at him move! Baby face or not, Fiona, you're looking at history."

"Oh, for heaven's sake, I'll be home when I'm home."

Both Fiona and Peter erupted in cheers.

"One nothing for us Dad."

Fiona heard her mother close the outside door.

"Hey Dad, wouldn't it be great to play in the NHL. Heck, I'd be happy just to play hockey here in the Memorial Arena. I love the sounds and the smell of the ice."

"Girls can't play hockey," Peter said gently. "Street hockey is one thing, forget about the arena."

"I wish I were a boy," Fiona said quietly.

"Come now, I don't." Peter said.

"But then you wouldn't tell me to hush and not think about it when I tell you how hard I imagine what it feels like skating fast down the ice, hair blowing behind you and Foster Hewit saying, 'He's split the defense. He shoots; he scores. What a fine play ladies and gentlemen!' Why is it wrong to imagine?"

"Give it up princess; it won't get you anywhere. Pay attention to the game now."

* * *

Fiona opened her eyes and stared at the ceiling. She heard the Bakers' car start. Fiona looked at her alarm clock. 10:00, must be time for church. Sunday. Fiona felt knife-like stabs in her stomach. The day of the big game and she couldn't play. She rolled on her stomach burying her face in the pillow hoping she could go back to sleep and wake up on Monday, hockey game over and she wouldn't even ask who won.

"Fiona, don't be a lazy bones; get out of bed." Jacqueline called just outside her door.

"In a minute," she answered.

"Fiona rolled herself deeper in her blankets knowing her feet would get cold as soon as she stepped out of bed. She heard the telephone ring.

"Fiona, it's for you."

"Coming." She got up and ran to the kitchen.

"It's Brenda."

"Hello."

"Fiona, Gary wants to talk with you; he's here...the guys thought your mom wouldn't let you talk if they phoned, so hang on a minute."

"Okay."

"Uh, Fiona?"

"Yeah."

"Is your mom listening?"

"Yeah."

"Just answer yes or no then. We guys thought, you know, like, since this was such a big game and everything, that we should make it real, and have a ref. So we took and vote and even George figured, like, you'd be the best person. Maybe if you're just, you know, reffing, your mom wouldn't get so mad, hey. So what do you think?"

"Uh, I don't know."

"C'mon Fiona, it's important; you know that."

"Oh, all right...but it's not what I want to do."

"Good. I'll tell Phil."

Sunday was cold all day. Fiona finished the Sunday dinner dishes. She put her coat and boots by the door. Jacqueline was playing her usual game of Solitaire in the living room. Peter was snoring. The Kraft man was giving a recipe on tv. Fiona put on her coat and as she closed the door on the warmth of the house, she could hear the slap slap of Jacqueline's cards and the Kraft man's voice as smooth as peanut butter, he was proclaiming.

Silence. She could hear the slight hum of the electrical meter. She walked down the driveway to the street, snow squeaking under her boots. She saw the guys down the road standing in a group. Waiting for her. This was the showdown.

"Fiona." Phil nodded to her and stepped on his cigarette.

"Okay, let's go," said George.

Gary paced out the perimeter of the rink, staying within the area of the street lamp.

"You know the rules," Phil said to the guys and handed Fiona the puck. "All we need you for is face offs and running after the puck if it goes out of bounds. We only have two tonight, so keep an eye on them."

"Okay." Fiona walked to the centre of the rink. Bobby and Wayne were picked to take the face off. Fiona dropped the puck and the game was under way.

Phil had the first chance to score, but put a wrist shot just wide of the jam cans. Fiona had run all the way to the Green's house two doors away to retrieve the puck. He had another chance after the next face off, but Raymond caught the puck in his baseball glove. George won the next face off and Fiona had to hex him real hard to make sure he missed his chance. Doug deflected the puck to the Riding's garbage can. It landed in a snow bank. They stopped the game to look for the puck. No one could find it. George reached into his coat pocket and brought out the other puck.

"Intermission between periods," said Phil.

The play went back and forth with no one scoring. Fiona kept wishing she could play instead of Kenny. She was better than him. And she could see that Raymond was weak on his left side. 'Low and to the left, I could score on him,' she thought, as she ran to get the puck. As she brought it back to the guys, she heard them talking in the distance.

"Great to have your own little groupie," said George.

"Yeah. Comes in handy when you need someone to get the puck. She'll do anything for us."

"Anything, Phil?"

Phil only smiled back.

As Fiona handed the puck back to Phil, she felt the anger start to burn in her. How could they! She was a hockey player, not a groupie. What was going on?

Bobby misdirected a shot past her feet. It hit the snow bank and careened all the way to her house. She just stood and watched it.

"Hey! Fiona!" The guys started yelling.

She watched them carefully; was going to refuse. Just then she heard Jacqueline's voice yelling in the distance.

"Fiona? FIONA!"

She started running towards her house.

"Aw jeez, it's her mother," she heard someone say. She reached the puck and picked it up.

"Here, go see your mother; I'll take it from here," Phil said as he caught up to her.

Fiona silently looked him straight in the eyes, then turned and kept running down the street.

"Hey!" Phil called. "Fiona, get back here."

"Fiona Louise!" she heard her mother's shrill yell behind her.

As she ran, her parka hood fell off her head. Fiona ran faster and faster. She was breathing great gulps of cold air. She ran as fast as she could. With her hood down, all she could hear was the roar of the wind in her ears. This is what hockey players hear. She thought of the roar of the crowd on Hockey Night in Canada. This is what they hear skating down the ice. She clutched the puck harder in her hand. She knew Phil was behind her; she ran faster and faster to the end of the street to the baseball field. There was nothing but snow covering it; no one had walked on the field for months. When she reached the edge, Fiona twirled like a discuss thrower—once, twice, three times around.

"A spin-a-rama. SHE SHOOTS; SHE SCORES!" Fiona yelled as she let go of the puck; watched it arc into the dark winter night.

Canine Pylons

John B. Lee

When I play hockey alone with my dog
in the moonlight
I'm Gretzky flashing circles round
a canine pylon.
He's there paw-splayed
turning and scrambling
and falling
and yelping for his skated-over tail.

But when he gets it
he can really carry the puck
in his mouth
and off the pond
into the snow
where he drops it
and it makes a round slot
plunking through onto frozen earth.
A dark needle in a white haystack
acres from the ice edge.

All the "Get it boy, get it boy,"
doesn't mean a thing.
He knows he's scored.
And somewhere
Foster Hewit has lost his voice from shouting
over barking dogs.
And somewhere Scott Young
is phoning in the scoop.
And somewhere dogs are laughing.
Somewhere that skates don't matter.
Somewhere that Wayne Gretzky
is just another pedestrian
walking four inches above the pavement.

When It Went Well
from *Bus Ride*
Don Gutteridge

When it went well it was like a dance. A shift to the right, all power channelled to that side, bursting back to the left, and the red jerseys, it seemed, merely playing their part in the intricate dance. One, down on his knees, unbelieving; a second, too clever, tangled in his own amazed skates. The speed was there now: red-line, three more jerseys behind him; the puck jumping to his muscled command. Net in sight, waiting, its role assured. Old feeling coming back; as if he could fly—skates like a breeze on the ice, speed alone would do it, would carry him up and over, he was rising, floating with the puck, into or over the goal, above the smothering applause, the suffocating snow, he was above it all, knowing the puck had found its own way, the applause secure, but high and floating now through the snow which had a beginning after all, here, high over it, floating and free with a peace shared only by a quiet cold audience of stars.

Such moments are reserved for our dreams. And we are probably poaching on Bill's private preserve, for it will be evident by now that the puck did go in the net, and Bill, rather than flying over the defence, simply skated past them and blasted a shot so powerful the Wanderers' goalie didn't move (on home-ice he would have made a suitable gesture, but why bother, here?) The first wave of anticipated applause, however, did not come, for young Bill, moving so fast, faster than anyone had seen him skate, seemed unable to stop, almost (they said after) as if he were in a trance, until the end-boards kindly untranced him. As soon as he stood up, shaken but unmarked, the cheers poured down from the heights of the five rows of bleachers.

Dream or reality, illusion or not, Bill had been flying, the old feeling in him. The exhilaration that only power and speed and youth can give. It was the reason, he had always thought, for those late afternoons on the marsh-ice below the River, for the Saturday mornings, winter and summer, shooting pucks at potato sacking till hand and eye become one motion, one will. And when there was no one to play against him, he would take a beaten-up kitchen chair and push it before him, hour after hour, till the calve-muscles ached and the ankle-bones rebelled long before his desire gave way and he limped home hurting all over. But dreaming of applause falling endlessly like snow around him; dreaming, too, of a real arena where every shift, every glistening shot, was rewarded with cheers, was recorded and sent winging on air-waves over all the snows of all this country's towns and hamlets.

Thin Ice

The Night the Arena Burned

Roger Bell

feet running feet pounding
out a message

voices

southern sky
unnightly orange

my feet join the urge
in us all
we race
the glowing
pulsing sky
pulling us
like blind night creatures
drawn closer to the searing light

and we slow to a lope
around the corner

ice white stars
and the blueblack between

the building roars
pained girders twist
anguished
curling up
  and falling
     and
     down comes the roof
we are bathed in heat

flame commands the darkness
and Sam says

"played a lot of hockey
            there" pauses
"from public school to rec league
sonofabitch" and sighs
            "we used to
pack the place
        Jerry Jerome and me
best defence to the rafters
fast ice sand floor
        back then
but jesus mother"
        his eyes bright

        "didn't that roof go down
            GREAT?"

Corner Man

Ted Plantos

If it's a fast
up
and down
game,
I'm lost

I can't keep up
Nothing worse

I don't skate
I struggle

I play
how I look,
broken nose
and all

I outwork
the opposition,
hustle in
the corners

I don't have the big ego
I know what I can
and can't do

I forget
how many time
my nose
get broken

I'm hit

with deflection
three game in a row

I broke
my jaw
in Chicoutimi
and had to wear
a mask after that

It's just a job
It feeds
my family

Even a guy like me,
he can do well

Come Back, Jesus, to the Hockey Game of Life

Roger Bell

Come back, Jesus,
from the sinbin
of Golgotha.
Your two long centuries
for gross misconduct
unbecoming a carpenter
are up; so says the clock,
and the fans want you back.
Come on, Jesus, think
of you and Bobby Orr
on the same team, and
Stanley Cups full of
the blood of your body
and bigger crowds
than the Sermon on the Mount.

(opening ceremonies
I can see it now
in lights—
Silly Graham, referee,
Oral Sex and Rex Humbug,
linesmen,
crowds singing,
"Butt-end for Jesus"
throwing fish and loaves)

Let's go, Jesus
Christ what a line—
H.G. on the left,
God playing centre ice,
and you on the right

with your famous holy shot
swift as a prayer
stickhandling through
Gentiles with that
great righteous cross.

Come out, Jesus!
Please us, Jesus!
Oh, wouldn't it be heaven?

Packing

Roger Bell

Nothing must be forgotten, this must be done slowly, carefully, purposefully:

First the towel, for when the game is over and your body pleads for the massage of steam and water. Then the two sweaters, the red then the white, always that order, you don't know why just do it, it came to you in a dream like a pass out of nowhere. Then the shin pads' long lean parabolas, the elbow pads tucked against one another like sleeping lovers, the gladiator helmet & cage where your brain will prowl, the shoulder pads folded left over right, always, the gloves, palms still soft and promising, one at each end to add some symmetry. Next the blue sweats, the t-shirt, the garter belt, the jock, the skate socks, the big socks striped and ready to contain. The pants' unwieldy armour. Then the skates, treat them kindly, with respect, they are your friends, they fit you and you alone like your fingerprints, you slide them into the side pockets then as you zip

look ahead concentrate:

Think of your winger, think of being in his skin breathing when he breathes, when he turns you go with him he is yours, if each man covers his own the system works.

Think of being shorthanded, think of long minutes playing the box four of you in perfect sync, keep the shooters to the outside outside is all motion no harm keep them from the slot keep the centre clean, make them pass time, don't even consider the other end your world has shrunk, just kill the clock stay in the square.

Think of line changes, prepare yourself, wait, watch for him to come off, brace your feet vault the boards hit the ice skating get both hands on your stick, measure the play look to your lines to appear be ready to say them like a mantra zip up the bag.

Now pick it up

over your right shoulder how many thousand times have you felt the weight shift? so you are ready for the tug then the drop steady your feet with your left hand pick up your sticks, heft them, feel the way they nestle into your welcoming grip, see the fresh black tape how it wraps and overlaps smoothed so no irregularities mar the way of the puck. Kiss your wife and children goodbye open the door

step out into a winter order

into the crisp predestined clarity of your vision.

The Goaltender is Missing
Roger Bell

I feel responsible, I was the last one to see him (alive? is left unspoken, no one wants to be the one to have the word brand his lips, it shows a lack of faith, and what is hockey, if not faith? I ask you).

3 a.m. I roll over, drugged with night, someone down the hall is screaming 'It's okay, it's okay, it'll never leave the room, you can trust us, we're your friends,' See? Trust. Faith. Followed by a thump, another yell, this one wordless, as if in exorcism.

His shadow occupies the chair by the curtained window. It is his eyes, aglow in a dark face that I see (or think I see, because this is now fast seeming a dream, I'm not sure I could or would swear to it). Goalies have those eyes, late into the night eyes feverous with self flagellation at the shot that trickled by, if only I'd played the angle better, kept my stick on the ice, stayed on my feet, anticipated, chose one, or all, goalies are tortured, their heads on endless loops that play and replay every movement into a slow freeze.

'Go to bed, it's late, big game in just a few hours.' My mouth barely working, maybe I don't say that at all, maybe I say 'What?' The face I can't quite discern responds 'I will, just let me finish this beer,' or maybe it doesn't, maybe what I hear is in goalie talk and can't be translated. I see a glinting tilt, hear an amber swallow, eager, and then I'm out, even the screamers now done, all that can be said, said, the weight of the day on them like wet sand.

Then it's day slapping me alive and the goalie is gone, I mean completely. Suitcase, equipment bag, car. Car! he was too drunk to walk, oh god, head-on family wiped out toys strewn, or upside down into deep rivers, or flattened against unyielding rock cuts, one wheel still spinning the evil slish of gasoline snaking to the hothot motor. The goalie is gone and a team without a goalie is no team at all. He is the crazy one, the one who chooses crucifixion, chooses the one on one the slap shot the tip the Horatio at the bridge aprés moi le deluge.

66

Out in this bright sun which tries its edge on my eyes the team has gathered to murmur, to speculate. I stand accused, it was my job to watch him, to guard the guardian when his guard was down, to save him from himself. But everybody knows goaltenders are unsaveable, it's their job to save. We huddle in the frost, stare at the space where his car sat, no one wants to say 'forfeit' but it's there, the clock is moving the sun rising the ice waiting.

The big defenceman stirs, I've seen him calm as poetry break up a four on one, we all defer to him, he says "We'll go to the arena, get dressed, take the ice if necessary, I know him, he'll be there." We all grasp this, like a stick thrown to you from the bench, your other lying shattered in the corner, the play leaving you. We as one, as the team turn towards the game, after all, what is hockey but turning your back on the goalie and knowing, what is hockey without faith? I ask you.

After, Driving Home

Roger Bell

Down the main street of Coldwater where big yellow nightmachines prowl and snow disappears into hungry trucks the adrenaline still like mad bees behind your eyes

over the stone bridge above the near frozen river the cold water steams at 26 below remember the speed limit   have to tell yourself to ease off ease off the gas the game is done try to make your right leg listen to the highway

first Fesserton where you are the only thing moving
Pink Floyd on the radio Hey! is there anybody
out there?
and a full moon rides high on your left, bothering only a few clouds tugging at their hems just the way you did, not so long before just the way you turned your stick into a suggestion to drag at the hip of the man flying by the play threatening to leave you behind your stickgesture judiciously reeling him in

on your right Matchedash Bay a frozen bulk nightwhite empty save for dark dots of fish huts an evening ellipsis

under the 400 overpass where big transports and faceless drivers rumble north you wonder are they tuned to Pink Floyd too and what they're carrying what is their burden and if they will go all the way on this song to the pacific rim of the world
and having there arrived this space music filling their cabs and washing into their heads like oceanswell drive off leaving the earth easily as spun molecules of thought

past Waubashene past the cemetery Anybody in there? some grave holds ephemera someone who like you used to strap on blades sharpalive What has spooked you? so that when the hitch hiker carved

from moonshadow leans up on the frosty shoulder do not stop you dare
not do not know what the driving mind may conjure on this lateness

hard around the 90 degree bend
then the yellow sign outside the OPEN AT 7 diner
you can almost almost the brown curl of bacon crunch of home fries
welcome eyes sunnyside up taste it soon soon if there is morning

out there you

must not allow yourself to become distracted Left
bypass Victoria Harbour a hillupdown past the old highway tunnel
where the wind plays weird coronet among flung synapses of ghost
headlights turn to Triple Bay Road cross where Port McNicoll tosses in
a dream and then you can sense the lake ahead speed upNo the music
is drifting across
the centre
line come back outside then
turn turn turn
or the black water has you then a few easy curves begin to let
yourself go slack
right to your street your house your driveway yawning

your wife still awake you want to tell her what it was like the game after
the puck dropped the way you tried to lose yourself but it's like a high-
way moonetched and stretched before you your highbeams pointing you
just put your foot
down and it just unravels the way you try

and so give up
you left all your best words   back there out there
on the road home

The North Field Comets

Allan Safarik

Things had seemed better than ever back in August when Orville and Del were putting together plans for the coming hockey season. They were shooting their weekly eight ball match over at the North Field Hotel. It was a tradition that had endured for over thirty years of Saturday afternoons.

"Should be a pretty fair team!" Orville thundered as he moved his belly around the cue.

Del, officially Delmar Fuchs, had been manager of the Comets since Moses was in prep school. "Well, Mayor," he intoned allowing a little shine to rub off on Orville, "with Wolf Slawson coming back to coach we'll be fast and mean."

Orville left the eight ball slightly off the rail near the far right hand end pocket. Del stepped up, tapped his cue toward the pocket and kissed the edge of the black ball with the white cue ball. The eight ball trickled off the table. Orville scratched his head, "How much do I owe you now?"

"Lemme see," Del said as he squinted into a pocket notebook. "Countin' these three games, you owe me a little under $382,000.00."

The news only got better. Racoon Coogle was over his broken leg. Billy Smiles, who was good for a goal a game, had just got out of jail. Thad MacDonald, nicknamed Onion Head, for obvious reasons had decided to put off retiring for another year. "What the hell, forty-four ain't too old and what'll I do all winter?" Onion Head, a slow stay-at-home defenceman, guarded the slot in front of his own net with the instincts of a wolverine. T-Bar Kelly, the flashy boy goalie was still working at the Petrocan. People were encouraged seeing him out behind the garage stopping shots. Best of all, Dwayne Semple had left the army and decided to return home to help farm with his Dad. Semple, a wiry offensive minded defenceman would lead the league in scraps and assists. He would be 'captain' because he would log the most ice time. Del was loving it. He could see the Wheatland Hockey League trophy glistening in its place of honour at the North Field Rink. Everyone figured having Wolf Slawson behind the bench was worth at least a one goal advantage. No referee in his right mind ever trifled with Wolf. All his great moments in life had occurred in the midst of mayhem on a sheet of ice. Fans on the road taunted him from across the rink. When Wolf's large lupine personality confronted them at close range they either meekly called him sir or wet their pants.

When Orville and Del drove over to Bluffsville for the annual Wheatland Hockey League meeting they knew trouble was brewing. League Commissioner, Aubrey Shanks, was a horrible homer who twisted league by-laws into his own personal agenda of justice. Shanks hosted the meeting in his barber shop. He waited until all the Governors were in place on the rickety wooden chairs beside the pile of Readers Digests.

Shanks had the hand of a beautician and a voice that could melt rust from car fenders. "Now boys, we'll have to have a small fee increase to cover the Commissioner's office."

They all listened politely and thought `why not?' Shanks' daughter Eloise took care of scheduling for eight teams and she kept statistics in her home computer. Mrs. Shanks took all the team pictures; handled league PR, and kept Shanks sober during the playoffs.

"One more thing," Shanks' voice took on a harsher tone and raised up in volume, "I'm not happy about Wolf Slawson coaching in this league. The man's demented. I told you boys from the Comets to get rid of him last year."

Orville and Del exchanged glances; they had been trying to sink Shanks for ten years. Del stood up. "Wolf's our coach, Aubrey. He behaved real good last year. Why there was only that one little incident when he bit that woman in Fairweather."

Orville chimed in with, "Yeah, while she was fixin' to clobber him with a length of pipe."

Shanks moved behind the barber chair. "Just so you know my feelings on Wolf, I'll suspend him fast if he even burps at a referee. By the way,

71

since you're all here, anybody need a haircut?"

Before the season started, Orville and Del took Wolf aside and told him to cool it. They figured the Comets would eat up the league, might as well save the rough stuff for the playoffs. Del thought of a slogan that Wolf could use to motivate the players. He got Polly to make a sign for the dressing room wall. It read, COMETS PLAY IT TOUGH, FAST, AND CLEAN. Orville and Del carried the sign over to the rink. The players were just coming off the ice after the first practice of the season. Billy Smiles was honking in the garbage can. Onion Head was unimpressed, "About as inspiring as the foaming cleanser," he remarked. Wolf left talking to himself.

By the end of the first month of the season the Comets were mired in a five game losing streak. In the first three games T-Bar played his heart out. The rest of the team were sluggish and unable to perform. Billy Smiles had lost his scoring touch. Raccoon Coogle's leg was killing him. In game four T-Bar with his butterfly style went into the toilet bowl, allowing four goals in less than three minutes of the second period. To make matters worse, Dwayne, who was fifth in league scoring had had his nose broken twice. Onion Head looked like he was skating in a cat-box. In game five, T-Bar was displaying lucky pink rabbit's feet attached to each of his leg pads. Wolf was pacing around in Del's storeroom like a wild animal in awful pain. Del was persuading him to try Slim in goal.

"It'll give the boys a different look, besides T-Bar's thinking too much and it might do him good to ride the pine."

"Okay, okay," Wolf agreed. "But if it don't work we do it my way."

Slim was a gamer, but the sound of his knees knocking together through his deer hair pads hardly inspired his teammates. The Black Blades from Bluffsville came into town and registered an 11-3 whipping to the Comets. They made it worse by gooning it up. Del and Orville said nothing when they encountered Aubrey Shanks smoking a foot long victory cigar in the rink lobby. Aubrey called it "A good old fashioned tuning."

Orville and Del were sitting in a corner booth at George's Cafe drinking coffee. George brought them the luncheon special.

"Here you go boys, two chop suey burgers. Anybody care for the catsup?"

Wolf Slawson came in stamping his feet from the cold and muttering 0 and 6 through clenched teeth. When George served him his coffee, Wolf was so distressed he tore the handle right off the cup. Del motioned for calm with his hand.

"Wolf," he said, "you're the coach; you call the shots from now on."

"Good," Wolf answered, "I've got a new slogan to put up in the dressing room."

"What is it?" Orville asked as he devoured half his hamburger.

Wolf's eyes glazed over and he answered, "IF IT'S MOVING, IT AIN'T DEAD."

George came out of the kitchen and sat at the booth. "I like it," he said. "It's catchy."

Wolf was a pack animal. He understood the old time pride of small town hockey players. First thing he did was grab T-Bar by the throat and take away all his lucky charms including the voodoo doll and the Playboy centrefold he tucked into his pads.

"No excuses," he said exhaling his bad breath between T-Bar's eyes. Wolf kicked over the coffee urn. He grabbed Billy Smile's lit cigarette and butted it into the palm of his hand. Turning on Racoon Coogle he sneered, "Coogle, that leg brace you're wearing would do more good if you wore it on your head." One by one he went around the room. When he got to Onion Head, he snorted, "You may as well head for the rest home the way you're playing." Wolf paused for a few frozen moments to let his tirade sink in. "We're gonna keep it simple. From now on, it's dump, chase, and staple. Anybody dare put the puck in our net ends up on the slab. Any questions?" There were none; everybody knew their duty. They had seen the weird light in Wolf's eyes before on the bitter winter night he went down after beating up the cops in Rosetown.

Naturally the Comets were more afraid of Wolf Slawson than they were of losing. They gave up the figure skating style that Del favoured and came out forechecking like demons. Onion Head, suffering from hurt feelings, began dealing out vicious hip checks at centre ice. Racoon Coogle threw away the leg brace and went on a scoring spree. T-Bar Kelly wanted to be loved more than anything. When Wolf growled in his face he got tunnel vision. The result was that the North Field Comets went on a 10 game winning streak. The whole town picked up. Orville was thinking about making a banner of the new slogan so they could display it on the bus. Del thought maybe they should wait and see how things went. Wolf was back to normal, barking at referees, stalking behind the bench like a zoo animal. T-Bar knew his luck had changed because of the four leaf clover he glued inside his right skate.

"Hello Del," this is Aubrey Shanks. "What the hell is going down in North Field?" Del held the phone out and let Shanks talk to the empty room. He knew Shanks was out of joint because the Comets were winning.

"I don't know what you're talking about," Del answered.

"The hell you do." Shanks was in a fury. "That moron Wolf Slawson threw a garbage can on the ice last night in Youngstown. Dumped in all over the linesman."

Del inquired cautiously, "Did the referee send in a report?"

"You know bloody well he didn't. First of all he was afraid of Slawson and second of all you boys from North Field smoothed him over after the game." Del left the receiver dangling and Shanks' ugly voice rasping in the rafters.

The Comets finished the regular season with 23 wins, 13 losses, and 2 ties. Their hopeless season had turned around. They easily qualified for the playoffs. In the first round of the playoffs they eliminated the Fairweather Honkers from post season play by taking the best of three in two games. All that stood between them and the Wheatland Cup was a three game series with the Bluffsville Blades. What was most galling to League Commissioner Shanks was that the Comets had earned the extra home game. Del and Orville had stopped talking to Shanks on the telephone. They knew that Wolf Slawson's methods had worked without degenerating too far into goon hockey. If things went right, the playoffs would remain without incident, at least until the final game. Once it came down to one shot for all the marbles Wolf might become an uncontrollable beast. His value as coach was the inspirational fear he raised in his own team and the terror his unpredictability caused in the opposition. Wolf was the kind of guy who liked to eat sardines right out of the can in the dressing room.

The Comets had a tradition. On game days against the Bluffsville Blades the bus left North Field at three in the afternoon. That way the team could stop half-way and have a pre-game meal together at Granny's Diner in Lonesome. Some of the players refrained from eating. T-Bar and Onion Head always had the dumplings with chicken liver gravy. The Bluffsville Blades also stopped at Granny's on their way into North Field. It was as if both teams needed to gather strength before entering enemy territory. After the game was over the visitors' bus would usually pull out and head for the Lonesome bar to avoid ugly incidents.

Orville nudged Del in the ribs at the end of the second period of the first playoff game. "Granny must be servin' some heavy food." The Comets playing at home had built up a 4 to zip lead.

Dwayne Semple was firing BB's from the point. They got in trouble in the third period when T-Bar started playing goal for the crowd instead of the team. His showboating resulted in two quick tallies at the ten minute mark. Then he juggled a long shot in the last minute and it dropped over his shoulder into the net. Wolf sent out five defencemen to kill off the final seconds. He instructed Onion Head to tell T-Bar if he let in another goal he would have his balls for a necktie.

Game two in Bluffsville was a different story. Several fights broke out in the crowd before the puck was dropped. Spit was raining down from overhead bleachers. During the first shift number 4 for the Blades, Boris Fistic, speared Dwayne Semple as he shifted the puck travelling through centre ice. Semple went down like a pole axed steer and was carried off to the dressing room. Onion Head attacked Fistic and got the extra five minutes for being the instigator. On his way to the penalty box he got into a fight with Bronco Provstski that got them both thrown out. The fans in Bluffsville were throwing pennies and the odd battery. Wolf was crouching on top of the boards like a snarling Doberman looking for a chance to leap onto the referee. When the smoke cleared the Comets were down 2 to 0. When the penalty was up Fistic went to his own bench and never left if for the duration of the game. Wolf began heckling Eagle Perkins, the Bluffsville coach, demanding that he put number 4 back on the ice. Eagle held his nose and made chicken sounds which drove Wolf into spasms of rage.

By the third period the game was lost. Bluffsville had a good power play and they filled the net in answer to Wolf's desire for revenge. The final score was Bluffsville 7, North Field 3. Now T-Bar Kelly was a flake, but not without reasons. When he saw Dwayne leave the game he knew that winning was in doubt. When Wolf attacked his pads between periods with a hockey stick T-Bar began to get tunnel vision. Every goal he let in burned in him like a hot poker. When the final buzzer sounded and after the obligatory pushing and shoving T-Bar slowly skated along the boards. He timed his arrival at the exit to coincide with that of Bluffsville's number 4. Inspired by some ungodly vision he lifted his stick like a double bladed axe and brought it down on Fistic's back. It took the Comets three hours to disentangle themselves form the brawl that ensued. Wolf chased Eagle Perkins three miles across a frozen Hutterite field before he gave up and trotted back to the bus. The North Field Comets and their fans stopped at the Lonesome Hotel on their way home. It was a mistake because two dozen hard core Bluffsville supporters following in cars rushed in and started another donnybrook.

The phone rang at 7 a.m.. "Hello, that you Del? Are you up?"

"Damnit, you know it Shanks. I open at 7:30."

Aubrey Shanks had waited up all night to make this call. His voice was thick as George's coffee. "Just wanted to let you know that gawdamn goofball hippy goalie of yours is suspended for the balance of the season for that unprovoked attack."

"Aubrey, aren't you being a little hasty. There was fault on both sides."

"Listen to me, Del," snorted Shanks, "he's suspended and now you've appealed and it ain't successful. So now you can live or die with Slim in the final game. Ha, ha. Good luck. Your whole town is full of bumheads and dumbsticks."

Later in the morning Del wandered over to the coffee shop. "Must have been quite a game," George remarked while cleaning off the table. Del filled the folks in on his conversation with Shanks.

Orville bounced his belly against the table, "That SOB is going to pay for insulting the good folks of North Field."

Del winced, "No time for a political speech. I guess we'll have to go with Slim in the nets next Friday night."

Orville lifted his eyebrows, "May as well mail Bluffsville the two points."

Problem was, after the brawl in Lonesome, Slim just disappeared into thin air. Wolf drove around town looking for him in the usual places. Finally, Slim's cousin Henry told Wolf that Slim had been called up to Edmonton to start a new job.

"He's sorry he won't be able to play in the big game."

Slim never had a job in his life. Henry was lucky Wolf was troubled by a hangover, or he might have had his throat ripped out. Del got on the phone to try and reason with Shanks. "Aubrey, we've been in this league a long time. These incidents have a way of being blown into full scale misunderstandings."

Shanks was eating a piece of Mrs. Shanks' Boston Cream pie while he conversed with Del. He smacked his lips at the end of his own sentences and swallowed when Del tried to speak. "That hippy dink goalie is out and that's that. But since Slim is out of town, I'll give you a break."

Del was waiting for this opportunity. "What kind of break?"

Shanks crooned back into the phone, "It wouldn't be fair to Bluffsville if you filled in with a ringer. But you can add to your roster any goalie who has ever been on it in the past."

Orville and Del were back sitting at George's along with Wolf and some of the players. They were scanning the rosters for the past twenty years looking for a goalie.

"Maybe we can get Tiny Simpson,"offered Onion Head.

Orville looked up, "Tiny had his leg amputated last year."

George remembered, "About five years ago there was a decent guy in nets."

"Yeah," Del remarked, "Chester Stonewall, but he's working on the oil rigs off Sable Island."

Smudge Peabody had been sitting in the corner reading his newspaper. "Don't mind me my two bits worth, but seems the town's got a big problem. Now there was only one goalie ever worth anything in North Field. The one and only Dutch Mowbray. Why he played six games for the Detroit Red Wings in '48 and all those years in the minor pro leagues."

Orville had come back from squeezing himself through the washroom door. "Dutch was a fine goalie in his day, but he was almost collecting his pension when he sat all those years behind Sawchuck."

Del looked up from the lists, "The only thing about it is that he qualifies because he played for the town from '66 through '69."

Smudge peered through the smoky room and said, "It's just like riding a bicycle. You never forget. Let's go out and talk to him."

Dutch Mowbray was changing the oil in his tractor when Orville, Del, and Smudge turned up at his barn door. "How you boys doin'? What can I do for you?" He stood before them in greasy overalls with a dark oil stain running through his yellowing white hair. On the bridge of his nose were the heaviest pair of glasses ever constructed.

Orville stuck his authority out, "We was just wondering if you ever hanker to get back in the net?"

"No, can't say that I miss it much," Dutch answered.

Del asked, "Guess there's a lot of pressure playing in the net and of course, with your eyesight being bad and all that, it would be risky."

Dutch put down his oily rag. "I'll tell you boys a little secret. I was successful because of my bad eyes."

"You don't say," Smudge offered.

"I never bothered looking at the puck. I played the angles. I figured

78

out where it was going by reflex rather than eyesight. In fact, I couldn't even see the puck when it was outside the blueline. It used to make me damn mad when I saw the little devil close up because that meant it was behind me. I loved the game, but hated the practising."

Coming out from the barn into natural light Del noticed the scars and dents that were magnified in Dutch's face, giving his lips a puckered look. Dutch went on, "Gave my pads away in '71 to the Simpson kid."

Del had just finished getting rid of Mrs. Cackleberry and her six kids who were running up and down the store's walls. The door chimes sounded and in walked Commissioner Aubrey Shanks.

"I heard the rumour that your birds are thinking about putting Dutch Mowbray in the nets on Friday night."

Del snapped back, "What if we are?"

"The League won't allow it on the grounds that he's a geriatric who might get hisself killed."

Del opened the desk drawer and pulled out his pile of ancient North Field rosters. "Here it is Shanks, in black and white. Mowbray, Dutch, goalie '66 to '69. Now you get out of town before Wolf Slawson finds out you're here and turns your ugly buttocks into dog food."

On Wednesday night Orville and Del sat disconsolate in the North Field Hotel beer parlour. "The biggest game of the year and we've got a 73 year old blind goalie." Del lifted his hand and waved for another round. Orville ordered two pickled eggs. Just when depression was getting the best of them, in swaggered Smudge Peabody.

"What you boys looking so down in the mouth about?" Smudge asked.

Del answered, "It's like this Smudge; we are plain worried that Dutch is liable to end up in the box on Friday night."

Smudge winked. "Won't happen if you don't let it happen."

"How's that?"

"I drove over to Lonesome and had supper at Granny's this evening. Not many people in there. Yesterday Aubrey Shanks and Eagle Perkins came in to plan the Friday night team dinner. Since Dutch'll be in the net they think the game is a foregone conclusion. They're planning on leaving Bluffsville early so they can have a fully catered team meal at Granny's before they move on to North field. And then a big bash later on after the game at the Lonesome Hotel."

Del looked a little green, "That's confidence for you."

"What do you mean if we don't let it happen?" wondered Orville.

"I mean just that," snickered Smudge. "We got an old man with grit in goal, but we need a bit of an edge. I chatted up Granny and she told me she gets Diane at the North Field Bakery to supply her desserts. Now everybody knows that young Ruby works all night at the bakery. Granny told me she ordered twenty-five Nanaimo Bars for Friday night."

2 a.m., Friday morning, Orville and Del pulled up in front of the North Field Bakery in Orville's Crown Victoria. They could see Ruby through the foggy picture window. Orville tapped with his car keys on the glass. Soon Ruby's face appeared and she went and opened the door.

"What are you doing here?" she asked.

Orville laughed and said, "Well, we was just going home from the bar and we thought we'd come by and get a snack."

"Come on in; I've got some coffee brewing in the back."

Orville and Del sipped coffee and munched on ginger snaps. "What's in the big mixer?"

"Oh, just the ingredients for a batch of Nanaimo Bars."

"That so?" said Del. "Quite a piece of machinery. Mind if I have a closer look?"

Half an hour later, Orville and Del bid Ruby goodnight.

"Well?" Orville asked impatiently. "How much did you manage to add?"

Del smiled, "I decided to go all the way. I threw in five packages of Ex-lax."

"No!"

"If you're gonna do something you may as well go all the way. Besides, only half of 'em will eat dessert, and that's all we need."

Orville beamed, "That Ruby's a swell cook."

Del laughed, "Hear she makes a hell of a Nanaimo Bar."

There was a lot of movement off the bus when the Bluffsville Blades arrived at the North Field Rink. The North Field fans were already gathering in front of the building. Some of them were screaming threats at the beleaguered Blades. Smudge was taking tickets at the door.

"Good evening boys, Eagle. How's it hanging, Aubrey?" Smudge was in his element searching their faces for a sign of weakness. Aubrey was carrying his dessert in a brown paper bag.

Eagle puffed himself up. "Had a good dinner and team meeting at Granny's; we're gonna be loose tonight!"

T-Bar was in the North Field dressing room helping Dutch Mowbray put on his hockey gear. Dutch stood there looking like an old tom turkey in his long johns. Wolf was bouncing off the walls telling the defencemen to play it tight and his forwards to shoot the bloody puck.

"We've got a pro in goal tonight, so let's not leave them on his doorstep."

Dutch finally got into his pads and put on his thick horn rim glasses. T-Bar was adjusting the straps on the goalie mask. Dutch looked at him, "Never wore one, never will. Damn things only block yer vision."

Del, standing behind Dutch said, "What the hell you talking about? Last Monday you told us you was blind, so what difference will it make? Put the damn mask on and save your life."

"Never has; never will. End of subject."

Del went over to Wolf to plead with him to talk Dutch into the mask. Wolf was already wearing his game face; he growled at Del and told him without words to get out of his room. Dutch reached out and put something on Del's hand. "Take good care of 'em. Mr. Adams bought 'em for me in '52." Del was holding a full set of dentures.

During the pre-game skate Dutch worked, scraping back and forth in the crease as if looking for some kind of miracle of traction. He stood nonchalantly facing shots from the point. When Dwayne whistled the puck by his ear he crossed himself and tucked his head further into his shoulders.

Onion Head skated over to him. "Do you want me to block the shot, or would you rather see it all the way?"

Dutch impatiently slapped his stick on the ice. "I don't exactly see the puck; I feel the shooter's motion."

In the lobby, Aubrey was making big jokes to Del and Orville. "I suppose you fellows pumped that old dude full of Geritol, huh? Hope he doesn't fall asleep in the middle of the game." With that comment, he unwrapped his Nanaimo Bar and washed it down with a cup of rink java.

"Well," says Orville, "I'm willing to put a little wager down on our boys tonight."

"That so?" says Aubrey. "How about a hundred bucks?"

"You're on."

The players went back into the dressing room while the Zamboni prepared the ice for the face off. Wolf was snarling at his defencemen. "If anybody goes one on one with Dutch, I'll be waiting here at the gate with my switchblade and you'll be singing falsetto. Remember, dump, chase, and staple. No fightin' till the third period and then only if we're out of it." Wolf began to pound his chest and howl like a wolf at the moon.

The North Field Comets came out of the dressing room like a pack of wolves. When they hit the ice the crowd went crazy. Dutch came out last and skated down to the wrong end of the rink. Onion Head, wielding his stick like a scythe among the black clad Blades, went down and retrieved him. Orville and Del, sitting in the poop deck over the south end, were watching the Bluffsville bench. Only about six of their players had come onto the ice; a few more were sitting with their heads down on the bench.

Aubrey was looking pretty shaky. "I'm feeling a little attack," he said.

82

"Just going to hit the washroom before the action starts."

In the first minute a puck deflected off a Comet player at centre ice and ticked onto Bronco Provotski's stick, giving him a clear break-a-way. He cruised in on Dutch, deking with his shoulder and his head. Dutch stayed motionless at the top of the crease. When Bronco veered across the front of the net to the backhand, Dutch stayed on his feet. Suddenly, his goalie stick recoiled like a cobra and he poke checked the puck off of Bronco's stick. By the time Aubrey returned from the john, the Comets, possessed by lupine tenacity, were swarming around the Bluffsville net. The score was already 2 to zip. In the rest of the period, Dutch faced only a long slap shot that hit him in the shoulder and ricochetted over the glass. Eagle Perkins had left the bench and gone back to the dressing room. Aubrey was no sooner sitting than he excused himself and went back for more. Orville and Del were living it up, cheering wildly.

"Good thing they're wearing their black uniforms," quipped Orville.

The Bluffsville bench could hardly manage a line change. When Aubrey appeared again the score was 5—0 and Bluffsville had iced the puck twenty-five times.

In the first intermission Dutch asked Onion Head, "Did that puck hit me?"

"No, that was the evening freight that ran into you. Didn't you see it coming down the track?"

Out in the lobby the crowd was pounding on the can door telling Aubrey to hurry up. He'd stagger out the door and go quickly to the end of the line.

"What's wrong, Shanks?" asked Smudge.

"Don't rightly know; I'm a touch under the weather."

Smudge offered Aubrey a Player's Filter.

"No thanks Smudge; I'm feeling a little peculiar."

"You know Aubrey, there's a real bad bout of influenza going around these days. Looks like you and your Bluffsville boys have caught it."

Aubrey was back in riding the porcelain bronco.

Meanwhile, Wolf, smelling blood, was going crazy in the dressing room. "Now is the time to hit everything that moves out there. Kill the body; the head dies."

The Comets came out hitting in the second period. Even when they were short handed they controlled the play. Dwayne Semple ragging the puck, saw an opening and headed straight for the Bluffsville net. Before he got there the Bluffsville goalie was headed for the bench.

"Easiest goal I ever scored," he said later in the bar. Dutch, playing the angles, stopped a half dozen shots sweeping the puck into the corners.

Wolf was screaming, "Kill number 4."

Boris Fistic was skating on his ankles using his stick like a rudder to help him navigate his own end. Wolf grabbed Onion Head at the bench and asked him why he wouldn't go in deep and nail him.

"Jeezus Wolf, get off my back; that guy smells like a septic tank."

By the third period Aubrey Shanks was walking as if he had the world's worst case of *ring of fire*. Eagle Perkins and the Bluffsville trainer were holding on to each other in the throes of gastric distress.

Smudge slapped Aubrey Shanks a little roughly on the shoulder and said, "Honestly Aubrey, your boys are skating tonight like they're carrying a load of lead in their pants."

Aubrey was in no position to argue. He opened his wallet and paid Orville the hundred dollars from the bet. Orville sent Del down behind the bench to tell Wolf that there was no need for a riot tonight.

"Wolf, those Blades are spent. Let 'em out of here with their lives." Wolf was still whining and shaking. Pleading for somebody, anybody to get even with Boris.

Aubrey presented the fabled Wheatland Cup to Del and Wolf and Dwayne in the world's shortest formal presentation. He excused himself and headed for the men's room. It was a long time before the Bluffsville Blades were able to crawl out of the dressing room to the safety of the bus. The rink lights had been turned off for an hour. Wolf Slawson had stayed outside the building howling like a madman, screaming at number 4 to come out and face the music. When he gave up and went to the celebration at the North Field Hotel, the Bluffsville team made their exit.

In the bar Onion Head stood up to make a toast. "This is for Dutch. Old and blind he may be; he never lost his touch."

The Hockey Player Sonnets

John B. Lee

i

What about them Leafs, eh!
(e.d.*) couldn't score an (e.d.) goal
if they propped the (e.d.'s) up
in front of the (e.d.) net
and put the (e.d.) puck on their (e.d.) stick
and the (e.d.) goalie fell asleep
and somebody (e.d.) yelled, SHOOT THE (e.d.) THING!
(E-E-E-E.D-eeeeeeee!!!!!!)

ii

(e.d.)!!this (e.d.) shower's (e.d.) cold.
who the (e.d.) flushed the (e.d.) toilet?
give me the (e.d.) soap.
hand me that (e.d.) towel.
has anybody got some (e.d.) shampoo?
toss the (e.d.) over here!
thanks. what's this (e.d.) pansy (e.d.)?

who brought the (e.d.) beer?
toss me one. stop throwing that (e.d.) snow.
you could lose an (e.d.) eye.
and so on...

iii

What do you mean you don't watch sports on TV.
Why the (e.d.) not?
Haven't you got an (e.d.) TV?

What the (e.d.) do you watch?
What the (e.d.) do you do?

Read!!!—who the (e.d.) wants to (e.d.) read!
too much like (e.d.) thinkin'.

there is much (e.d.) laughter at this.
and so it goes—
'what about them Leafs, eh...'

  (*expletive deleted)

My First Hockey Service

Mick Burrs

I feel like an alien from a desert planet where no one skates, where ice is a mirage, and where the closest thing to pucks are camel droppings. It's my first live hockey game in Canada. Or should I say: my first hockey service.

Here I am, sitting on one of the green benches in the bleachers near centre ice under a heater that isn't working, frigid air rising from the cement floor into the soles of my boots. I'm a visitor at the Al Ritchie Memorial Arena in Regina, Saskatchewan. And this is a late night clashing the day after Christmas, 1980.

I huddle among hockey parents, secular worshippers in their community sanctuary. They've come to watch their cherubs in uniform play in the bantam league, the Cougars versus the Lions.

But I'll soon be given reason to believe that it's really the Christians versus the Lions. Because tonight is the night I'll discover: hockey is not exactly in the same league as Sunday School.

On the bench in front of me, a hockey mother makes a verbal appeal for divine intervention: KNOCK HIS GODDAMN BLOCK OFF! ICE THE FUCKIN' THING!

So help me, she's got a babe against her breast and—WHERE TH' HELL DIDJA LEARN TA PLAY THIS GAME, YA FUCKIN' CHRYSANTHEMUM!

This modern madonna, Our Hockey Mother of the Curses, is chewing a wad of gum and holding an unlit cigarette in her free hand. Beautiful.

Another hockey mom is sitting beside me. She hardly says anything, watches silently, one could even say morosely.

Who is enjoying this service anyway?

The young players all look grim and determined, as if they were taking a mathematics exam. Their coaches resemble men who have just lost their jobs and are facing divorce, bankruptcy, and a fatal disease all in one swoop. And the adults in this congregation don't exactly sit there clapping their hands, smiling and laughing, looking serene.

Between the first and second period, nearly everyone leaves the bleachers to get a shot of coffee in a styrofoam cup, or to smoke a cigarette. but this is bantam hockey: no fights, no violence. Not like what I see on television where the heroes of these young guys are all gods who use their sticks and their gloves and their flashing skates to express something other than brotherly love.

To make sure, however, that I don't leave this place with any wrong impressions about hockey's holy appeal and the primary expectations of its devoted worshippers, I watch some older kid not wearing a uniform walk onto the ice immediately after the service is over.

He punches a player in the face.

Hey, it's Boxing Day. Against all ritual the losing team is instructed not to shake the winning team's hands.

Having also achieved the proper spirit of this earthly religion, I frown as I walk out. I feel like I'm leaving a funeral parlour.

I have no illusions. I know this is a sacred sport played and watched in every city and village in Canada. It has winners and losers who all pray fervently for grace and violence and victory. But now you can see why I am also assured: they don't play hockey in heaven.

Taking Your Baby to the Junior Hockey Game

Don McKay

Watch for it to happen out there on the ice:
this music they fight for.
You can feel her beside you as though poised in front of the net
circling
circling.

Christ, you'll say,
baby if you were a forty-three-year-old Montreal potato merchant
I'd be your five iron.
I would never dissolve, in the middle of a rush, passes
coming snap snap crossing the blue line barely on-side, never
dissolve into adolescence fumbling
for control.
I would cleave
I would be your hawk
I would be silence.
Forests.
And baby, you'll say, if you conducted the Bach Society Choir
                    in town
I'd be a dentist's wife
straining among sturdy contraltos after your unheard perfection
longing with them to devour your wrists, your boyish wit.
I would finish your every mad flight through the defence
with deft flicks to the lower-left and upper-right-hand corners,
inevitable, the momentary angel,
your right wing.

Dreamskaters

Don McKay

,chasing chance with all the moves
of swallows swirling to
connect, their physics
liquified by knives, carving and
releasing from the ice the cold
caught music of the river, stroke, stroke,
just have time to scribble you this note then
scissor and wheel synchromesh to long
parabolas of sense they pour and
drink their speed those
tossed off phrases those
sky readers those high
raptors

Kosher Leaf

for Shel

John Tyndall

Shmuel's beloved Zaida
grew to love watching
after Motze Shabbat
his favourite player
on Hockey Night in Canada
number fourteen Dave Keon
my favourite player
before Sabbath Day
not only my Maple Leaf hero
Lady Byng's gentleman also
became Zaida's mensch

The Hockey Game

Laurence Hutchman

Before the face-off
of the Toronto-Montreal game
he begins talking.

—Yes, I have been here a few years,
you know I am Polish...After the war
I spent five years in Siberia.

—It was below zero in winter.
We had to cut wood in the daytime.
At night we slept in tents.

—I was strong then,
now I feel pain in my shoulders
when you are young it doesn't...

—Because I told the truth,
some normal thing in conversation,
I was taken away.

Ice shines brightly on his glasses
players flash across his vision
through red circles and blue lines.

—I am an optometrist, now.

He smiles, cheers.

For good hockey,
a good game.

The Feminine

Richard Harrison

My plan for a deck of hockey Tarot cards failed for want of the truly feminine. I could make some figure a woman in the game; Canada's women's team is the best in the world, and maybe I could push the notion until it does not matter, woman or man—just The Player. But I'd be lying. This is not why I love the game, or why its symbols work like runes in my language. This is a game the women watch, its gentler moments taken in their image: The Trainer, running to the Fallen Man Beside the Boards, cradling the face now loose and looking skyward in his hands, smoothing his hair with a towel; the Equipment itself, stockings, girdles, garters. At the time I did not understand what the woman next to me at a hockey game was trying to teach when she wondered aloud whether she would find a better lover in another woman as the players below us skated the warm-up, around and around their own side of Centre, lofting long, lazy Pucks at their Goalie. There is a Mask on my face, the game divides us. Again I've come to a profession of love in words I cannot use for you, with all the women left in the stands where I demand that you sit and love it all.

All-Time Game

Richard Harrison

One on one we are drafting the all-time game between us my brother and I, not the Official All-Time Team of Six with no one to play; we are truly opposed, the language inflated and gross the way men talk when they mean it pretending they don't. The Big Six are all English which I say reflects the voters. Then I say I could beat those guys with Lemieux, Robitaille, Richard up front; Bourque & Savard at the blueline. Plante in net. He says we should draft for the ultimate game, and the heavy checkers come out of our mouths, the policemen, and our finest players get banged up along the boards. The game deteriorates; because he nearly killed a man, I pick Eddie Shore. It's like this over table hockey, us at each other, huge pucks in the tiny nets, the anger of 30 years, everything out of proportion.

The Sweater

Richard Harrison

Could I tell you he was beautiful, returned from winter camp in a sweater really from the team whose crest it bore, him standing among us with our hands outstretched; I touched the cloth. Shall I tell you of his smile, his reckless arms that day; in a hockey town he was a son in his father's own colours, how the son once called his favourite teacher coach and the father, meeting that teacher, took his thin, long hand in his huge fingers, enfolding it in inescapable size and said my son loved you! Shall I speak of the love then, too? a black suit burning gold at the edge; in the middle of class this young man held up his arm in a sleeve of Stanley Cups.

Thin Ice

Betsy Struthers

All of us play at reconciliation,
a game of shinny on the backyard rink,
where bluelines shadow thin ice:

You and me and your daughter
against our husbands and my son.
Last year, it was family vs family

when you were still a family. (Now
it's two on one, power plays, goals
missed and disputed.)

Thwack of stick on stick, the shush of skates:
your husband crouched, ready to glove
any shot you try to get by him.

The kids have given up, cold feet, fed up
with the fights, you at one end, he
at the other, the two of us

circling between you, unwilling
to be audience or referees.
You've also had enough,

but he isn't ready to quit. The surface
chips under our blades, brings us
to our knees. Call it a draw

if you want. Or a victory. Whatever
it's time to be done with this, admit
that it's over

Bob Skates

John B. Lee

When the boys were young
and Christmas season came
white to the windward side of half-sheltered bushes
and the parlour
smelled of pine
we made the error
of purchasing skates.
For the older son
a pair of black leather Bauers
in a box
and for the younger
a pair of pewter-coloured bobs
you strap to shoes
like slip shods.
The second he saw them
he took and hurled them strap by strap
across the festive room
so they clattered snapping in the corner
for even at three
he would rather have been a weed
stuck in the ice
than have worn those mocking things
just once.

Swallowing Pride

Don Gutteridge

The papers said
they couldn't build
a rink big enough
to swallow his pride

My Dad: on skates and
over ice that was
ground, a gravity
giving speed, a
moving not of its own
but a boy on blades
making wings out of
legs arms the heart
swelling thru every
muscle drew
order out of energy
design from the
chaos of the game

With a stick held
like a brand
he burned the puck
beyond the net
the circling boards
the crowd's containment
beyond the
    perfection of applause
he soared on wings
the ice gave only
to the young and once:

Icarus on blades
the world
    his rink.

Northland Pro

Gary Hyland

My father said the Northland Pro was the world's finest hockey stick. This back when I was shorter than the boards on the outdoor rink and he was still skating for the Hornets. That's when he bought his only Northland. Mother cursed it—a sliver of wood worth more than half a ton of coal.

He showed me how to judge the lie, the grain, the splice, the shaft for flex and strength, how to space and roll the tape and seal it, sizzling, on the stove. To keep the moisture out, he varnished it, then stood it, perfect and golden, by his equipment in the spare room. At night when he was at work, I'd creep in and hold it, so incredibly light and balanced, smell the mix of varnish, tape and wood and feel the hat tricks flying from its blade. Too beautiful to ice with the cheaper hacking sticks, the gouging of steel.

Each year, even after he'd hung up his skates and I was playing on the high school team, he'd sip beer, add another coat of varnish and talk to that Northland about what they could have done and might yet do. But he got stuck on night shifts and rye and never did see me play, even after he retired, the curved blade and fibreglass days. When he died, the Northland passed to me. It sits in the closet of my den, and once a winter, even now that I've hung up my skates, I open a beer, take it out, dust the darkening wood, and tell it what we might have done.

Daddy is a Monkey

Mark Cochrane

quips my son, gap-toothed
from his fall on the ice, a whole person
glistening from his eyes
to mine, hiccuping

giggles at his own joke,
just two-&-a-half
with a toy chimp stuffed
into a helmet & jersey
& playing in the slot

between his grampa—my father—& me
on the sofa, as we dangle
from the final seconds
of the Kings' game, an arena
where we can still meet, Dad reaching out
across space
and *his* father's pocket-watch, arranged
like a trophy on the hutch,
to caress my arm—

an awkward
animal grooming
in the glade of his apartment,
neither of us possessing
speech for this—

his opposable thumb in the hair
above my wrist
where the blood warms,
soothed & confused by the same touch

that tended me
when i was the boy who loved him
full in the face
as a child will allow
for only so long: full
& unmasked, without a helmet
painted with a crown, & free
from the dread of any loss, sudden
or slow, even
as the clock was running down.

That Sign of Perfection

C.H. (Marty) Gervais

Pity—it would have
been *nice* having our pictures
framed together: me a youngster
from Bracebridge, Ont., sporting
the proud Canadiens sweater, he,
my son, sharing the glitter
of the famed Punch Line
& carrying visions of Rocket Richard
in our boyish eyes & terribly
thin arms. But no! Instead
there he is, a bullheaded
six-year-old wearing that
damn Toronto Maple Leaf
sweater, shooting down
the ice like a tin garbage
can, arms & legs in all
directions. I yell after him,
"Keep that head up! Don't
look at your feet!"
Then recall my own novitiate
in that frigid northern arena,
wheeling in circles on the
gray ice, worried sick over
the moment when someone
would notice how the leather
insteps of my skates had
been ground to sawdust
from skating on my ankles.
"Keep that head up!" & watch
the endless hours fade into
memory as he attempts time

103

after time to stop with
a spray of ice, just like
the hockey players on trading
cards, one foot raised
over the other, but time &
again he tumbles into
the boards. I see me in him
playing till daylight fades
into darkness & we stickhandled
our shadows into goals & glory.
I see him in me, driving on,
searching for some hope of
perfection, that blazing instant
when the skate blades glint
in the afternoon like
silver rockets & when the
black disc tumbles lightly
into the twine.

A Career In Hockey

A Career in Hockey

Robert Hilles

i

I was never much good at hockey. One of the few games I played was against the Hudson family from across Longbow Lake. We cleared a part of the bay near our house and used tomato juice cans weighed down with rocks as goal posts. Our fathers played goal and we didn't have much equipment, so they were outfitted with a broom and baseball glove. They both looked like players confused about the game they were playing, dressed for a cross between curling and baseball. The Hudson brothers were much better skaters than my brother and me. We could hardly skate at all in fact. I didn't own a pair of skates and had to flop around the ice in my gum boots. It was then I learned that they didn't stick to ice worth a damn and I was left flailing about trying to keep my feet from giving way under me and at the same time fighting for the puck. The brothers were hard body checkers too, knocking my bother and me into the snow bank several times. Once my head struck something hard in the snow and I saw stars for a moment before my brother yanked me back to the game. I returned just in time to see one of the Hudson brothers heading towards our net with a clear break. My father looked so alone there, his back to the open lake behind him. It wasn't like the hockey games I'd seen on TV where the goalie was protected by the boards behind him with the fans looking on from the safety of the crowd. Behind my father, only the still open water, menacing over his left shoulder. I can see him clearly, standing so tall ready to defend that small bit of ice as if it were the one thing in life all his own. I'm trying to keep my father alive on the page, even as he struggles on in Winnipeg with his cancer. His career in hockey, like mine, was nothing more than a few images preserved in the shrinking maze of his thoughts. I never saw the puck go past him, my gaze already lowered at my feet. I found my face peering back at me reflected in the dark ice, and I put my hand down to feel it, as the Hudson brothers celebrated another goal some-

106

where, just behind me, while my father chased across the lake for the puck. As I tried to grab a hold of my face trapped in the ice, I thought about fleeing towards that open water, not to plunge, but to stand at the edge and drop the puck. I knew the puck would never sink, rather it would simply float crazily on the surface taunting me to jump in. When I looked up again, leaving my face where it was in the ice, my father was handing my brother the puck. He looked handsome, as he stood proudly with his broom and glove. With the broom, he brushed off the snow that clung to his pants. Wet patches revealed where the heat of his body had begun to melt the snow. I expected to see steam coming off his pants, but there were just the frequent bursts of fog from his mouth as his warm breath caught air and light. He was warming the world a little bit at a time with his breathing. Those same lungs are filled with cancer now, and I wish I had a better picture of that day. Not this fragile construction of words. But I have none, just as there is no record of the score. All is gone, except for the image of my father waving his broom wildly to distract the shooters, his head held confidently in the sun, the day firmly around him like the smiling faces of his sons, each chasing the puck in his own crazy fashion, keeping it away as best he could from his father's crude net. Funny, I can't remember the other father or brothers, beyond how it felt to be checked into a pile of snow, but my brother and father are so clear to me I could reach out and take their passes even now. Our careers in hockey were highlighted by that short game. The sun followed the play from overhead, spreading its rays for us across the rippled ice. Out in the middle of the lake, open water waited for the spring we still protected deep inside. For now, the game was not over yet.

ii

When I was in grade four, I used to stand against the cement wall of Central school and let the other boys raise pucks at me. I wore no protective equipment. All I had was my goalie stick and my bare hands. Even though it seems like a crazy thing to do, when I think back, I'm still proud I did it. It was one of the few times I wasn't afraid. Some of the pucks would careen off a shin, a shoulder, or the top of my head. Miraculously, I was never hurt nor cut, though I performed this feat every day for a whole spring. I think now of the boys who stood in line to shoot pucks at me. What was the pleasure they got in practising against someone who caught pucks with his bare hands? I know, at the same time, it was the kind of thing that boys did then. Still do. It's what drives them to hockey in the first place. The grace of the game transforms them. Through the complicated twists and turns the player finds in his body, the skeleton of an angel. Those on the ice with him saw it too, and no matter how hard or rough the game got, the rest of the world drifted away from him and when he returned to it, he was changed. I stood proudly against the wall and faced every shot they made, never ducking, catching many of them in my bare hand, the flesh stinging for a second or two before I flung the puck back to the next waiting shooter. After a while, I learned I could detect things in their eyes as they faced me that they weren't aware of, that gave me a little hint of where they were telegraphing the shot. They would be shocked to see me reach out a hand to where the puck would be even before it left their stick. I felt brave and not the small boy who had gotten so used to being picked on. I don't wish to be standing against a wall again, facing shots, but I do long for that moment when I could see in another's eyes what he thought no one else could see. The longer I faced the shooters, the longer the line got—each boy in the schoolyard wanting to have a try at me. Perhaps in my imagination, an NHL scout was at the edge, watching me, not yet realizing myself that he wouldn't be interested in such a display, especially from any boy who couldn't skate. Near summer, the palm on my right hand had calluses from all that rubber, and at night I would rub my palm before I'd go to sleep taking pride in how a part of my body had learned to harden against the world. By the next fall, I had tired of the game and gone on to other things. But no one came to take my place against the wall. No one was that crazy or desperate. Like me, they had all taken to watching small men on a tv screen scurry across the ice like wild animals afraid to be out in the open.

In phys-ed class I once had to play a hockey game even though I had only skated once before in my life. Since I was so slow, they put me on defence. But my playing that position didn't last long because the first body check I got, knocked me out. After recuperating on the bench for awhile, I was put into goal. I liked it there. It was so quiet most of the time. You could watch the flurry of activity at the other end and smile at the play so far away it could have been on television. Once, a tall red-headed boy from another class had a break away against me, and even with my eyes closed, I was able to stop the puck. I looked at it as lifeless as a stone in my glove. Calmly, I let it drop to the ice as if I knew what I was doing, imitating something I'd seen Johnny Bower do. The game went back to the opposing end again and I could dream for awhile. From my vantage it looked so odd when our team scored, arms lifting in the air before any muted cheer reached me. A goal was just as invisible from far away as it was from close in, as if in that brief moment when the puck crossed the goal line everyone had their eyes closed. At that moment, I knew my career in hockey was over. I've never played a game since, not even road hockey. I still watch our national sport on tv where every goal scored is so well documented it's easy to forget that scoring is actually a very quiet, invisible thing. The event of scoring, or being scored upon, passes before you know it. What does get remembered is what occurs next—players jumping around cheering, the crowd going wild, as if out in the dark winter somewhere a god might have observed, turning away from his work to note the wonder.

My father told me, recently, he'd always wanted a career in baseball not hockey. He preferred baseball because it was played in the summer. In the dead of winter, the sky did something dangerous to your eyes as it reflected off the snow. I never once saw him play baseball and must be satisfied to imagine him playing short stop, whizzing between bases to prevent a hit going beyond infield. In hockey, I imagine him playing defence, even though the only position I ever saw him play was goal. He's never been fond of being indoors. Perhaps that's why he prefers baseball. I think often about him giving up his dreams for his children—how parents did a lot more of that then. I don't admire it as much as admit that it scares me. In my mind, I can see him catching fly balls in the big open field at Smith's farm where he grew up. The ball would have been doing things in the air that his hands knew about, his shoulders turning in time to keep his balance. Later, he told me he played out in an open field by Redden's Camp and that he was fast on his feet. His position was first base, his hands smothering a line drive quicker than a frog's tongue snaps a fly. I see the quickness in his hands even now, the cancer treatments making him jumpy, his eyes avoiding the sun too much. In winter, they cleared the ice on Longbow Lake and played hockey until the ice got too thin for them. He wasn't that fast on skates, and his ankles were weak like mine. The ice surface so uneven you could break an ankle just turning in your own end. Hockey and baseball stop you from climbing into yourself, the light freeing different parts of you. His career in hockey was better than mine, and I see, looking back, it is best to keep dreams hidden. I would have liked to have seen him play in his youth. The few photographs I stumbled across this summer are the only ones I have of him as a teenager. And I want to be standing in the same room with that young man, seeking and finding in his smile how the world began. On the cold ice, he must have been quicker than he admits, his self-conscious laugh catching me over the phone. It's possible to have a career in hockey, whether others notice or not. Perhaps my father's career out on a cold lake in the bush of northern Ontario is the real, preferred career. It was the kind he could look back on and still dream. The wind crossed his face while he lumbered down the ice. As he breathed in, his body began to sail out over the lake with a sudden burst of speed and he found himself alone facing the open lake before him, and if he'd been able to, he'd have let himself fly away.

v

My brother lost his two front teeth falling in a hockey game on Longbow Lake. The next day I found the map of blood his accident had left behind. I reached down and touched the dried blood bonded to the cold surface. His blood's heat must have melted away some of the ice, because I noticed a small dip. A little of the blood came off on my warm hand. I tasted it and smiled. He'd been checked from behind, his face jammed to the ice, and when he turned back to the game, his face revealed a bloody, toothless grin. He never collected the missing teeth, but left them there on the ice. When I went back for them they were gone and I wasn't sure if he'd returned for them or the wind had blown them under a cover of snow. For twenty years, he went toothless in front and he was proud of his dark smile. Only recently has he gotten a bridge to fill in the gap. He never played hockey much after that day. His stick stayed exactly where he'd left it on the porch. Several times my mother went to throw it out, but stopped herself without knowing why. My brother finally took it with him when he moved out, though I've never seen it at his new place. His career, like mine, never outlasted more than one or two hockey sticks, the number a slapsure NHL'er might use in a single game. Our sticks were made of wood and we wrapped them with electrical tape. That day when he fell, he could have gotten up and whacked the culprit, but he never did. He just got back into the flow. By the end of the game, the blood had dried on his face. Later, my mother washed it off with a warm cloth, sobbing as she did, and my brother never stopped smiling the whole time. The light in his eyes made him look braver than he truly was, and he knew it—his hand raised half way to his shoulder as if he still held that damn stick.

vi

The kids in town skated on well-groomed rinks, but I preferred our cleared patch of ice on the lake. When I go back to Kenora, it's always in summer. I try to envision where the ice was cleared on the surface of

111

the lake, but I can't. The water stops me. I reach for a handful of that clear liquid and try to cup its cold in my palm, but I can't. It pours easily through the small spaces between my fingers. All the same, I love how it catches the light as it falls and I can see the ice hidden in the liquid flow.

The lake's surface is so much smoother when it is covered in ice. Even if the freeze is rough. After I gave up skating for good, I would come down to the lake to watch from the bank while those who were good on skates played. As I followed their moves, my eyes were half closed from the glare. I knew if I closed them completely, all the skaters would disappear, leaving the game behind us like my father and I had done. Their careers in hockey remembered only by the skate and stick marks they'd left on the frozen surface where the ice dreamed its way back to water.